Chanting from the Heart

Chanting from the Heart

VOLUME 1

BUDDHIST SUTRAS AND CHANTS FOR RECITATION

Thich Nhat Hanh
and the
MONKS AND NUNS
of PLUM VILLAGE

PARALLAX
PRESS

BERKELEY, CALIFORNIA

Parallax Press
2236B Sixth Street
Berkeley, California 94710
parallax.org

Parallax Press is the publishing division of
Plum Village Community of Engaged Buddhism

Calligraphy by Thich Nhat Hanh and Brother Phap Huu
Cover design by Gopa & Ted2, Inc. based on
an original design by Charles Woods and Ayelet Maida
Text design by Gopa & Ted2, Inc.

Discourses translated from Pali retain Pali spellings.
Discourses translated from Chinese retain Sanskrit spellings.

ISBN: 978-1-952692-37-6
E-book ISBN: 978-1-952692-38-3

Library of Congress Cataloging-in-Publication Data
is available upon request.

1 2 3 4 5 / 27 26 25 24 23

Contents

CHANTS

Introduction

CHANTING FROM THE HEART, VOLUMES I AND II, is a collection of verses, chants, practices, and ceremonies, developed and used regularly by the monks, nuns, and laypeople at the monasteries and lay retreat centers established by Vietnamese Buddhist Zen Master Thich Nhat Hanh and his community (in France, the USA, Thailand, Hong Kong, Germany, and Australia). The book was first published in the year 2000. It is in the main a translation of a chanting book compiled and composed by the Venerable Thich Nhat Hanh in Vietnamese. Throughout his life he composed and translated from Chinese into Vietnamese ancient Buddhist scriptures. This is a new revision in two volumes. The first volume contains sutras and chants, and the second volume contains the ceremonies and other formal practices, a musical notation section, and a glossary.

INTRODUCTION TO VOLUME 1,
BUDDHIST SUTRAS AND CHANTS FOR RECITATION

In this volume you will find sutras which you can recite in sangha gatherings or during your personal practice sessions at home. You can read them aloud or to yourself. Inserted in the text you will see the word [BELL] at intervals. This is a point where you can pause and breathe mindfully without thinking about anything in order for your heart to receive the meaning of what you have just read.

Because these are sutras for reading aloud, they have sometimes been abbreviated from the originals in the Chinese and Pali canons, omitting the many repetitions, which are usual in the originals. This does not detract from the meaningful content of the sutra. The complete versions of the sutras along with commentaries by the Venerable Thich Nhat Hanh are available in many cases in books published by Parallax Press.

All of the sutras here are translated from the Vietnamese of the Venerable Thich Nhat Hanh who translated them from Chinese or Pali. Many were published in the Vietnamese chanting book *Nhat Tung Thien Mon* in 2012. Some sutras were more recently translated and distributed during Dharma talks in Plum Village in 2013 and 2014.

Most of the sutras belong to the category of "deep meaning" (*liao yi* in Chinese). You may not understand them all at once. So take your time and let them penetrate your mind slowly.

May these words of Shakyamuni Buddha water the seeds of the good, the beautiful, and the true in your consciousness.

True Virtue
Plum Village, France
2023

Discourses

Discourse on Love

"Someone who wants to attain peace should practice being upright, humble, and capable of using loving speech. They will know how to live simply and happily, with senses calmed, without being covetous and carried away by the emotions of the majority. Let them not do anything that will be disapproved of by the wise ones.

"(And this is what they contemplate:)

"May everyone be happy and safe, and may their hearts be filled with joy.

"May all beings live in security and in peace—beings who are frail or strong, tall or short, big or small, visible or invisible, near or far away, already born or yet to be born. May all of them dwell in perfect tranquility.

"Let no one do harm to anyone. Let no one put the life of anyone in danger. Let no one, out of anger or ill will, wish anyone any harm.

"Just as a mother loves and protects her only child at the risk of her own life, let us cultivate our love to offer to all living beings in the entire cosmos. Let our boundless love pervade the whole universe, above, below, and across. Our love will know no obstacles. Our heart will be absolutely free from hatred and enmity. Whether standing or walking, sitting or lying, as long as we are awake, we should maintain this mindfulness of love in our own heart. This is the noblest way of living.

"Free from wrong views, greed, and sensual desires, living in beauty and realizing perfect understanding, those who practice boundless love will certainly transcend birth and death."

Metta Sutta, Sutta Nipāta 1.8*

---

*For commentary, see Thich Nhat Hanh, *Teachings on Love* (Berkeley, CA: Parallax Press, 1998).

Discourse on Happiness

I heard these words of the Buddha one time when the Lord was living in the vicinity of Savatthi at the Anathapindika Monastery in the Jeta Grove. Late at night, a deva appeared whose light and beauty made the whole Jeta Grove shine radiantly. After paying respects to the Buddha, the deva asked him a question in the form of a verse:

"Many gods and men are eager to know
what are the greatest blessings
which can bring about a peaceful and happy life.
Please, Tathagata, will you teach us?"

(This is the Buddha's answer:)

"Not to be associated with the foolish ones,
to live in the company of wise people,
and to honor those who are worth honoring—
this is the greatest happiness.

"To live in a good environment,
to have planted good seeds,
and to realize that you are on the right path—
this is the greatest happiness.

"To have a chance to learn,
and to be skillful in your profession or craft,
and to know how to practice the precepts and loving speech—
this is the greatest happiness.

"To be able to support your parents,
to cherish your own family,
and to have a job that you like—
this is the greatest happiness.

"To live in accord with the Dharma, to be generous in giving,
to be able to give support to relatives and friends,
and to live a life of blameless conduct—
this is the greatest happiness.

"To avoid doing what is unwholesome,
to avoid being caught by alcoholism or drugs,
and to be diligent in doing good things—
this is the greatest happiness.

"To be humble and polite,
to be grateful and content with a simple life,
and not to miss the occasion to learn the Dharma—
this is the greatest happiness.

"To persevere and be open to change,
to have regular contact with monks and nuns,
and to participate in Dharma sharing—
this is the greatest happiness.

"To live diligently and attentively,
to perceive the Noble Truths,
and to realize nirvana—
this is the greatest happiness.

"To live in the world
with your heart undisturbed by the world,
with all sorrows ended, dwelling in peace—
this is the greatest happiness.

"Those who accomplish this,
will remain unvanquished wherever they go,
always they will be safe and happy—
Happiness is found within oneself.

Mahāmangala Sutta, Sutta Nipāta 2.4*

---

*For further commentary, see *Two Treasures: Buddhist Teachings on Awakening and True Happiness* (Berkeley, CA: Parallax Press, 2007).

Elder Discourse

I heard these words of the Buddha one time when the Lord was staying at the monastery in the Jeta Grove, in the town of Shravasti. At that time there was a monk named Thera (Elder), who always preferred to be alone. Whenever he could, he praised the practice of living alone. He sought alms alone and sat in meditation alone.

One time a group of bhikshus came to the Lord, paid their respect by prostrating at his feet, stepped to one side, sat down at a distance, and said, "Blessed One, there is an elder by the name of Thera who only wants to be alone. He always praises the practice of living alone. He goes into the village alone to seek alms, returns home from the village alone, and sits in meditation alone."

The Lord Buddha told one of the bhikshus, "Please go to the place where the monk Thera lives and tell him I wish to see him."

The bhikshu obeyed. When the monk Thera heard the Buddha's wish, he came without delay, prostrated at the feet of the Buddha, stepped to one side, and sat down at a distance. Then the Blessed One asked the monk Thera, "Is it true that you prefer to be alone, praise the life of solitude, go for alms alone, come back from the village alone, and sit in meditation alone?"

The monk Thera replied, "It is true, Blessed One."

Buddha asked the monk Thera, "How do you live alone?"

The monk Thera replied, "I live alone; no one else lives with me. I praise the practice of being alone. I go for alms alone, and I come back from the village alone. I sit in meditation alone. That is all."

The Buddha taught: "You are indeed someone who likes to live alone. I do not want to deny that, but I know a truly wonderful way of living alone. It is the way of looking deeply to see that the past no longer is and the future has not yet come, and to dwell at ease in the present moment, free from desire. When practitioners live in this way, they have no hesitation in their heart. They give up all anxieties and regrets, let go of all binding desires, and cut the fetters which prevent them from being free. This is called 'truly living alone.' There is no more wonderful way of being alone than this."

Then the Blessed One recited this gatha:

"Looking deeply at life,
seeing clearly the nature of all objects of mind,
not caught in any of them,
leaving behind all craving and attachment,
living in peace and joy like that
is to live alone."

Hearing the Lord's words, the monk Thera was delighted. He prostrated respectfully to the Buddha and departed.

Samyukta Āgama 1071
(The equivalent in the Pali Canon is
Theranamo Sutta, Samyutta Nikāya 21.10*)

---

* For commentary, see Thich Nhat Hanh, *Our Appointment with Life* (Berkeley, CA: Parallax Press, 1990).

Discourse on Knowing the Better Way
To Live Alone

I heard these words of the Buddha one time when the Lord was staying at the monastery in the Jeta Grove, in the town of Savatthi. He called all the monks to him and instructed them, "Bhikkhus!"

And the bhikkhus replied, "We are here."

The Blessed One taught, "I will teach you what is meant by 'knowing the better way to live alone.' I will begin with an outline of the teaching, and then I will give a detailed explanation. Bhikkhus, please listen carefully."

"Blessed One, we are listening."

The Buddha taught:

> "Do not pursue the past.
> Do not lose yourself in the future.
> The past no longer is.
> The future has not yet come.
> Looking deeply at life as it is
> in the very here and now,
> the practitioner dwells
> in stability and freedom.
> We must be diligent today.
> To wait till tomorrow is too late.
> Death comes unexpectedly.
> How can we bargain with it?
> The sage calls a person who
> dwells in mindfulness
> night and day
> 'the one who knows
> the better way to live alone.

"Bhikkhus, what do we mean by 'pursuing the past'? When you consider the way your body was in the past, the way your feelings were in the past, the way your perceptions were in the past, the way your mental formations were in the past, the way your consciousness was in the past; when you consider these things and your mind is burdened by and attached to these things which belong to the past, then you are pursuing the past.

"Bhikkhus, what is meant by 'not pursuing the past'? When you consider the way your body was in the past, the way your feelings were in the past, the way your perceptions were in the past, the way your mental formations were in the past, the way your consciousness was in the past; when you consider these things but your mind is neither enslaved by nor attached to these things which belong to the past, then you are not pursuing the past.

"Bhikkhus, what is meant by 'losing yourself in the future'? When you consider the way your body will be in the future, the way your feelings will be in the future, the way your perceptions will be in the future, the way your mental formations will be in the future, the way your consciousness will be in the future; when you consider these things and your mind is burdened by and daydreaming about these things which belong to the future, then you are losing yourself in the future.

"Bhikkhus, what is meant by 'not losing yourself in the future'? When you consider the way your body will be in the future, the way your feelings will be in the future, the way your perceptions will be in the future, the way your mental formations will be in the future, the way your consciousness will be in the future; when you consider these things but your mind is not burdened by or daydreaming about these things which belong to the future, then you are not losing yourself in the future.

"Bhikkhus, what is meant by 'being swept away by the present'? When someone does not study or learn anything about the Awakened One, or the teachings of love and understanding, or the community that lives in harmony and awareness; when that person knows nothing about the noble teachers and their teachings, and does not practice these teachings, and thinks, 'This body is myself; I am this body. These feelings are myself; I am these feelings. This perception is myself; I am this perception. This mental formation is myself; I am this mental formation. This consciousness is myself; I am this consciousness,' then that person is being swept away by the present.

"Bhikkhus, what is meant by 'not being swept away by the present'? When someone studies and learns about the Awakened One, the teachings of love and understanding, and the community that lives in harmony and awareness; when that person knows about noble teachers and their teachings, practices these teachings, and does not think, 'This body is myself; I am this body. These feelings are myself; I am these feelings. This perception is myself; I am this perception. This mental formation is myself; I am this mental formation. This consciousness is myself; I am this consciousness,' then that person is not being swept away by the present.

"Bhikkhus, I have presented the outline and the detailed explanation of knowing the better way to live alone."

Thus the Buddha taught, and the bhikkhus were delighted to put his teachings into practice.

Bhaddekaratta Sutta, Majjhima Nikāya 131*

---

*For commentary, see Thich Nhat Hanh, *Our Appointment with Life* (Berkeley. CA: Parallax Press, 1990).

Discourse on the Four Kinds of Nutriments

This is what I heard one time when the Buddha was in the Anathapindika Monastery in the Jeta Grove near to the town of Shravasti.

That day the Buddha told the monks: "There are four kinds of nutriments which enable living beings to grow and maintain life. What are these four nutriments? The first is edible food, the second is the food of sense impressions, the third is the food of volition, and the fourth is the food of consciousness.

"Bhikkhus, how should a practitioner regard edible food? Imagine a young couple with a baby boy whom they look after and raise with all their love. One day they decide to bring their son to another country to make their living. They have to go through the difficulties and dangers of a desert. During the journey, they run out of provisions and fall extremely hungry. There is no way out for them and they discuss the following plan: 'We only have one son whom we love with all our heart. If we eat his flesh we shall survive and manage to overcome this dangerous situation. If we do not eat his flesh all three of us will die.' After this discussion, they killed their son, with tears of pain and gritting their teeth they ate the flesh of their son, just so as to be able to live and come out of the desert."

The Buddha asked: "Do you think that couple ate their son's flesh because they wanted to enjoy its taste and because they wanted their bodies to have the nutriment that would make them more beautiful?"

The monks replied: "No, Venerable Lord." The Buddha asked: "Were the couple forced to eat their son's flesh in order to survive and escape from the dangers of the desert?" The monks replied: "Yes, Venerable Lord."

The Buddha taught: "Monks, every time we ingest edible food, we should train ourselves to look at it as our son's flesh. If we meditate on it in this way we shall have clear insight and understanding, which puts an end to misperceptions about edible food, and our attachment to sensual pleasures will dissolve. Once the attachment to sensual pleasures is transformed there are no longer any internal formations concerning the five objects of sensual pleasure in the noble disciple who applies themselves to the training and the practice. When the internal formations still bind us we have to keep returning to this world.

"How should the practitioner meditate on the food of sense impressions? Imagine a cow which has lost its skin. Wherever it goes the insects and maggots which live in the earth, in the dust, and on the vegetation attach themselves to the cow and suck its blood. If the cow lies on the earth, the maggots in the earth will attach themselves to her and feed off her. If she goes down into the water, the insects in the water will attach themselves to her and feed off her. If she stands in the open space, the insects in the air will attach themselves to her and feed off her. Whether lying down or standing up, the cow will be irritated and suffer pain. When you ingest the food of sense impressions, you should practice to see it in this light. You will have insight and understanding which puts an end to misperceptions concerning the food of sense impressions. When you have this insight you will no longer be attached to the three kinds of feeling.* When no longer attached to the three kinds of feeling, the noble disciple does not need to strive anymore because whatever needs to be done has already been done.

"How should the practitioner meditate on the food of volition? Imagine there is a village or a large town near to a pit of burning charcoal. There are only the smokeless, glowing embers left. Now there is an intelligent man with enough wisdom who does not want to suffer and only wants happiness and peace. He does not want to die and he only wants to live. He thinks: 'Over there the heat is very great, although there is no smoke and there are no flames. Still, if I have to go into that pit there is no doubt that I shall die.' Knowing this he is determined to leave that large town or that village and go somewhere else. Practitioners should meditate like this on the food of volition. Meditating like this they will have insight and understanding which puts an end to misperceptions about the food of volition. When they arrive at that understanding the three kinds of craving† will be ended. When these three cravings are ended, the noble disciple who trains and practices will have no more work to do, because whatever needs to be done has already been done.

"How should the practitioner meditate on the food of consciousness? Imagine that the soldiers of the king have arrested a criminal. They bind him and bring him to the king. Because he has committed theft he is punished by people piercing his body with three hundred knives. He is assailed by fear and pain all day and all night. Practitioners should regard the food of consciousness in this light. If they do they will realize a clear insight and understanding of the food of consciousness. When they have

*Pleasant, painful, and neutral feelings.
†Sensual pleasures, existence, and nonexistence.

this insight and understanding about the food of consciousness, then they will realize insight and clear understanding about the psychesoma. When they have insight and clear understanding about the psychesoma, noble disciples who train and practice will not need to strive anymore because whatever needs to be done has been done."

When the Buddha had spoken, the monks were very happy to put the teachings into practice.

Samyukta Āgama, Sutra 373*

---

*For commentary on this sutra, see Thich Nhat Hanh, *The Mindfulness Survival Kit* (Berkeley, CA: Parallax Press, 2014).

Discourse on the Middle Way

I heard these words of the Buddha one time when the Lord was staying at the guest house in a forest of the district of Nala. At that time, the Venerable Katyayana came to visit him and asked, "The Tathagata has spoken of Right View. How would the Tathagata describe Right View?"

The Buddha told the venerable monk, "People in the world tend to believe in one of two views: the view of being or the view of nonbeing. That is because they are bound to wrong perception. It is wrong perception that leads to the concepts of being and nonbeing. Katyayana, most people are bound to the internal formations of discrimination and preference, grasping and attachment. Those who are not bound to the internal knots of grasping and attachment no longer imagine and cling to the idea of a self. They understand, for example, that suffering comes to be when conditions are favorable, and that it fades away when conditions are no longer favorable. They no longer have any doubts. Their understanding has not come to them through others; it is their own insight. This insight is called Right View, and this is the way the Tathagata would describe Right View.

"How is this so? When people who have correct insight observe the coming to be of the world, the idea of nonbeing does not arise in them, and when they observe the fading away of the world, the idea of being does not arise in their mind. Katyayana, viewing the world as being is an extreme; viewing it as nonbeing is another extreme. The Tathagata avoids these two extremes and teaches the Dharma dwelling in the Middle Way.

"The Middle Way says that this is, because that is; this is not, because that is not. Because there is ignorance, there are formations; because there are formations, there is consciousness; because there is consciousness, there is the psyche-soma; because there is the psyche-soma, there are the six senses; because there are the six senses, there is contact; because there is contact, there is feeling; because there is feeling, there is craving; because there is craving, there is grasping; because there is grasping, there is becoming; because there is becoming, there is birth; because there is birth, there are old age, death, grief, and sorrow. That is how this entire mass of suffering arises. But with the fading away of ignorance, formations cease; with the fading away of formations, consciousness ceases . . . and finally birth, old age, death, grief, and sorrow will fade away. That is how this entire mass of suffering ceases."

After listening to the Buddha, the Venerable Katyayana was enlightened and liberated from sorrow. He was able to untie all of his internal knots and attain arhatship.

Samyukta Āgama 301*

---

*For commentary on this sutra, see Thich Nhat Hanh, *Beyond the Self* (Berkeley, CA: Parallax Press, 2010).

Anuradha Discourse

I heard these words of the Buddha one time when the Lord was staying in the gabled house in the Great Forest near the town of Vesali. At that time, the Venerable Anuradha was staying in a hermitage in the forest not far from where the Buddha was. One day a group of recluses came to see the Venerable Anuradha, and after exchanging greetings and courtesies, asked the venerable monk, "Venerable Anuradha, the Tathagata is often praised for having reached the highest fruit of awakening. He must have explained to you his understanding of these four propositions:

1. "After death, the Tathagata continues to exist.
2. "After death, the Tathagata ceases to exist.
3. "After death, the Tathagata both continues and ceases to exist.
4. "After death, the Tathagata neither continues nor ceases to exist.

"Please tell us which of these propositions is true."

The Venerable Anuradha replied, "Friends, the Tathagata, the World-Honored One, the one who has realized the highest fruit of awakening, has never proposed or spoken about these four propositions."

When they heard the Venerable Anuradha's reply, the recluses said, "It is possible that this monk has just been ordained, or if he was ordained some time ago, he must be of slow wits." Not satisfied with Venerable Anuradha's answer, they left him.

When the recluses had gone, the Venerable Anuradha thought, "If recluses continue to ask me these questions, how should I answer so as to speak the truth and not misrepresent the teachings of the Buddha? How should I answer so as to be in harmony with the right Dharma and not to be criticized by the adherents of the Buddha's path?" Then Anuradha went to where the Buddha was staying, bowed to the Buddha, spoke words of greeting, and then told the Buddha what had happened.

The Buddha asked him, "What do you think, Anuradha? Can you find the Tathagata in form?"

"No, World-Honored One."

"Can you find the Tathagata outside of form?"

"No, World-Honored One."

"Can you find the Tathagata in feelings, perceptions, mental formations, or consciousness?"

"No, World-Honored One."

"Can you find the Tathagata outside of feelings, perceptions, mental formations, or consciousness?"

"No, World-Honored One."

"Well then, Anuradha, do you think that the Tathagata transcends form, feelings, perceptions, mental formations, and consciousness?"

"No, World-Honored One."

"Anuradha, if you cannot find the Tathagata even while he is still alive, can you find the Tathagata within these four propositions:

1. "After death, the Tathagata continues to exist.
2. "After death, the Tathagata ceases to exist.
3. "After death, the Tathagata both continues and ceases to exist.
4. "After death, the Tathagata neither continues nor ceases to exist."

"No, World-Honored One."

"Quite so, Anuradha. The Tathagata has only taught in relation to one thing: suffering and the end of suffering."

Samyutta Nikāya 22.86

Discourse on the Full Awareness of Breathing

I

I heard these words of the Buddha one time when he was staying in Savatthi in the Eastern Park, with many well-known and accomplished disciples, including Sariputta, Mahamoggallana, Mahakassapa, Mahakaccayana, Mahakotthita, Mahakappina, Mahacunda, Anuruddha, Revata, and Ananda. The senior bhikkhus in the community were diligently instructing bhikkhus who were new to the practice—some instructing ten bhikkhus, some twenty, some thirty, and some forty; and in this way the bhikkhus who were new to the practice gradually made great progress.

That night the moon was full, and the Pavarana Ceremony was held to mark the end of the rainy-season retreat. Lord Buddha, the Awakened One, was sitting in the open air, and his disciples were gathered around him. After looking over the assembly, he began to speak:

"O bhikkhus, our community is pure and good. At its heart, it is without useless and boastful talk, and therefore it deserves to receive offerings and be considered a field of merit and worthy of respect.

"O bhikkhus, there are bhikkhus in this assembly who have realized the fruit of arhatship, destroyed every root of affliction, laid aside every burden, and attained right understanding and emancipation. There are also bhikkhus who have cut off the first five internal knots and realized the fruit of never returning to the cycle of birth and death.

"There are those who have thrown off the first three internal knots and realized the fruit of returning once more. They have cut off the roots of greed, hatred, and ignorance, and will only need to return to the cycle of birth and death one more time. There are those who have thrown off the three internal knots and attained the fruit of stream-enterer, coursing steadily to the awakened state. There are those who practice the Four Establishments of Mindfulness. There are those who practice the Four Right Efforts, and those who practice the Four Bases of Success. There are those who practice the Five Faculties, those who practice the Five Powers, those who practice the Seven Factors of Awakening, and those who practice the Noble Eightfold Path. There are those who practice loving kindness, those who practice compassion, those who practice joy, and those who practice equanimity. There are those who practice the Nine Contemplations, and

those who practice the observation of impermanence. There are also bhikkhus who practice Full Awareness of Breathing."

II

"O bhikkhus, Full Awareness of Breathing, if developed and practiced continuously, will be rewarding and bring great advantages. It will lead to
success in practicing the Four Establishments of Mindfulness. If the Four
Establishments of Mindfulness are developed and practiced continuously,
it will lead to success in the practice of the Seven Factors of Awaking. The
Seven Factors of Awakening, if developed and practiced continuously, will
give rise to understanding and liberation of the mind.

"What is the way to develop and practice continuously Full Awareness
of Breathing so that the practice will be rewarding and offer great benefit?

"It is like this, bhikkhus: the practitioner goes into the forest or to the
foot of a tree, or to any deserted place, sits stably in the lotus position,
holding their body quite straight, and practices like this:

'Breathing in, I know I am breathing in. Breathing out, I know I am
  breathing out.'
'Breathing in a long or short breath, I know I am breathing in a long or
  short breath. Breathing out a long or short breath, I know I am breathing out a long or short breath. They practice like this.
'Breathing in, I am aware of my whole body. Breathing out, I am aware
  of my whole body.' They practice like this.
'Breathing in, I calm my whole body. Breathing out, I calm my whole
  body.' They practice like this.
'Breathing in, I feel joyful. Breathing out, I feel joyful.' They practice like
  this.
'Breathing in, I feel happy. Breathing out, I feel happy.' They practice
  like this.
'Breathing in, I am aware of the mental formation. Breathing out, I am
  aware of the mental formation.' They practice like this.
'Breathing in, I calm the mental formation. Breathing out, I calm the
  mental formation.' They practice like this.
'Breathing in, I am aware of my mind. Breathing out, I am aware of my
  mind.' They practice like this.
'Breathing in, I make my mind happy. Breathing out, I make my mind
  happy.' They practice like this.

'Breathing in, I concentrate my mind. Breathing out, I concentrate my mind.' They practice like this.

'Breathing in, I liberate my mind. Breathing out, I liberate my mind.' They practice like this.

'Breathing in, I observe the impermanent nature of all dharmas. Breathing out, I observe the impermanent nature of all dharmas.' They practice like this.

'Breathing in, I observe that no phenomenon is worthy of craving and attachment. Breathing out, I observe that no phenomenon is worthy of craving and attachment.' They practice like this.

'Breathing in, I observe the no-birth, no-death nature of all phenomena. Breathing out, I observe the no-birth, no-death nature of all phenomena.' They practice like this.

'Breathing in, I observe letting go. Breathing out, I observe letting go.' They practice like this.

"Full Awareness of Breathing, if developed and practiced continuously according to these instructions, will be rewarding and of great benefit."

III

"In what way does one develop and continuously practice Full Awareness of Breathing, in order to succeed in the practice of the Four Establishments of Mindfulness?

"When the practitioner breathes in or out a long or a short breath, aware of their breath or whole body, or aware that they are making their whole body calm and at peace, they abide peacefully in the observation of the body in the body, persevering, fully awake, clearly understanding their state, gone beyond all attachment and aversion to this life. These exercises of breathing with full awareness belong to the First Establishment of Mindfulness, the body.

"When the practitioner breathes in or out, aware of joy or happiness, of the mental formations, or to make the mental formations peaceful, they abide peacefully in the observation of the feelings in the feelings, persevering, fully awake, clearly understanding their state, gone beyond all attachment and aversion to this life. These exercises of breathing with Full Awareness belong to the Second Establishment of Mindfulness, the feelings.

"When the practitioner breathes in or out with the awareness of the mind, or to make the mind happy, to collect the mind in concentration, or to free and liberate the mind, they abide peacefully in the observation of the mind in the mind, persevering, fully awake, clearly understanding their state, gone beyond all attachment and aversion to this life. These exercises of breathing with Full Awareness belong to the Third Establishment of Mindfulness, the mind. Without Full Awareness of Breathing, there can be no development of mindfulness and understanding.

"When the practitioner breathes in or breathes out and contemplates impermanence or that no phenomenon is worthy of craving and attachment, or the no-birth, no-death nature of all phenomena, or letting go, they abide peacefully in the observations of the objects of mind in the objects of mind, persevering, fully awake, clearly understanding their state, gone beyond all attachment and aversion to this life. These exercises of breathing with Full Awareness belong to the Fourth Establishment of Mindfulness, the objects of mind.

"The practice of Full Awareness of Breathing, if developed and practiced continuously, will lead to perfect accomplishment of the Four Establishments of Mindfulness."

IV

"Moreover, if they are developed and continuously practiced, the Four Establishments of Mindfulness will lead to perfect accomplishment of the Seven Factors of Awakening. How is this so?

"When the practitioner abides in the practice of observing the body in the body, the feelings in the feelings, the mind in the mind, and the objects of mind in the objects of mind, diligent, fully awake, clearly understanding their state, gone beyond all attachment and aversion to this life, at that point mindfulness is maintained in a sustained and steadfast way, and they will attain the First Factor of Awakening, namely mindfulness. With cultivation this factor will in time come to fulfilment.

"When the practitioner abides in mindfulness and can contemplate and investigate objects of mind, then the Second Factor of Awakening will be born and developed, the factor of investigating objects of mind. With cultivation this factor will in time come to fulfilment.

"When the practitioner abides in the contemplation and investigation of objects of mind in a sustained, diligent, and steadfast way, the Third Factor of Awakening will be born and developed, the factor of energy. With cultivation this factor will in time come to fulfilment.

"When the practitioner abides in the practice of diligence in a sustained and steadfast way, the Fourth Factor of Awakening will be born and developed, the factor of spiritual joy. With cultivation-this factor will in time come to fulfilment.

"When the practitioner can abide in the state of spiritual joy, they will feel their body and mind light and at peace. At this point the Fifth Factor of Awakening will be born and developed, the factor of ease. With cultivation this factor will in time come to fulfilment.

"When both body and mind are at ease, the practitioner can easily enter into concentration. At this point the Sixth Factor of Awakening will be born and developed, the factor of concentration. With cultivation this factor will in time come to fulfilment.

"When the practitioner is abiding in concentration they will cease discriminating and comparing. At this point the Seventh Factor of Awakening will be born and developed, the factor of equanimity. With cultivation this factor will in time come to fulfilment.

"This is how the Four Establishments of Mindfulness, if developed and practiced continuously, will lead to perfect accomplishment of the Seven Factors of Awakening."

V

"How will the Seven Factors of Awakening, if developed and practiced continuously, lead to the accomplishment of understanding and liberation?

"The practitioner cultivates the Seven Factors of Awakening, living in quiet seclusion, meditating diligently on the non-desirable and no-birth, no-death nature of all things in order to perfect the ability to let go. That is how the cultivation and development of the Seven Factors of Awakening will lead to the accomplishment of understanding and liberation."

VI

This is what the Lord, the Awakened One, said; and everyone in the assembly felt delight at having heard his teachings.

Ānāpānasati Sutta, Majjhima Nikāya 118*

---

*For commentary, see Thich Nhat Hanh, *Breathe! You Are Alive: Sutra on the Full Awareness of Breathing* (Berkeley, CA: Parallax Press, 1995) and *Path of Emancipation* (Berkeley, CA: Parallax Press, 2000).

Discourse on the Four Establishments of Mindfulness

I

I heard these words of the Buddha one time when he was living at Kammassadhamma, a market town of the Kuru people. The Buddha addressed the bhikkhus, "O bhikkhus."

And the bhikkhus replied, "Venerable Lord."

The Buddha said, "Bhikkhus, there is one way to help living beings realize purification, overcome directly grief and sorrow, end pain and anxiety, travel the right path, and realize nibbana. This way is the Four Establishments of Mindfulness.

"What are the Four Establishments?

"Bhikkhus, a practitioner remains established in the contemplation of the body in the body, the feelings in the feelings, the mind in the mind, and the objects of mind in the objects of mind, diligent, with clear understanding, mindful, having abandoned every craving and every distaste for this life."

II

"And how does a practitioner remain established in the contemplation of the body in the body?

"They go to the forest, to the foot of a tree, or to an empty room, sit down cross-legged in the lotus position, hold their body straight, and establish mindfulness in front of them. They breathe in, aware that they are breathing in. They breathe out, aware that they are breathing out. When they breathe in a long breath, they know, 'I am breathing in a long breath.' When they breathe out a long breath, they know, 'I am breathing out a long breath.' When they breathe in a short breath, they know, 'I am breathing in a short breath.' When they breathe out a short breath, they know, 'I am breathing out a short breath.'

"Just as a skilled potter knows when he makes a long turn on the wheel, 'I am making a long turn,' and knows when he makes a short turn, 'I am making a short turn,' so a practitioner, when they breathe in a long breath, know, 'I am breathing in a long breath,' and when they breathe in a short breath, knows, 'I am breathing in a short breath,' when they breathe out a long breath, knows, 'I am breathing out a long breath,' and when they breathe out a short breath, knows, 'I am breathing out a short breath.'

"They train themselves as follows: 'Breathing in, I am aware of my whole body. Breathing out, I am aware of my whole body. Breathing in, I calm my body. Breathing out, I calm my body.'

"Moreover, when a practitioner walks, they are aware, 'I am walking.' When they are standing, they are aware, 'I am standing.' When they are sitting, they are aware, 'I am sitting.' When they are lying down, they are aware, 'I am lying down.' In whatever position their body happens to be, they are aware of the position of the body.

"When the practitioner is going forward or backward, they apply full awareness to their going forward or backward. When they look in front or look behind, bend down or stand up, they also apply full awareness to what they are doing. They apply full awareness to wearing the sanghati robe or carrying the alms bowl. When they eat or drink, chew, or savor the food, they apply full awareness to all this. When passing excrement or urinating, they apply full awareness to this. When they walk, stand, lie down, sit, sleep or wake up, speak or are silent, they shine their awareness on their own body.

"Further, the practitioner meditates on their very own body from the soles of the feet upwards and then from the hair on top of the head downwards, a body contained inside the skin and full of all the impurities which belong to the body: 'Here is the hair of the head, the hairs on the body, the nails, teeth, skin, flesh, sinews, bones, bone marrow, kidneys, heart, liver, diaphragm, spleen, lungs, intestines, bowels, excrement, bile, phlegm, pus, blood, sweat, fat, tears, grease, saliva, mucus, synovial fluid, urine.'

"Bhikkhus, imagine a sack which can be opened at both ends, containing a variety of grains—brown rice, wild rice, mung beans, kidney beans, sesame, white rice. When someone with good eyesight opens the sack, they will review it like this: 'This is brown rice, this is wild rice, these are mung beans, these are kidney beans, these are sesame seeds, this is white rice.' Just so the practitioner passes in review the whole of their body from the soles of the feet to the hair on the top of the head, a body enclosed in a layer of skin and full of all the impurities which belong to the body: 'Here is the hair of the head, the hairs on the body, nails, teeth, skin, flesh, sinews, bones, bone marrow, kidneys, heart, liver, diaphragm, spleen, lungs, intestines, bowels, excrement, bile, phlegm, pus, blood, sweat, fat, tears, grease, saliva, mucus, synovial fluid, urine.'

"Further, in whichever position their body happens to be, the practitioner passes in review the elements which constitute the body: 'In this body is the earth element, the water element, the fire element, and the air element.'

"As a skilled butcher or an apprentice butcher, having killed a cow, might sit at the crossroads to divide the cow into many parts, the practitioner passes in review the elements which comprise their very own body: 'Here in this body are the earth element, the water element, the fire element, and the air element.'

Further, the practitioner sees a corpse thrown onto a charnel ground and lying there for one, two, or three days—bloated, blue in color, and festering, and they contemplate this truth as regards their own body, 'This body of mine is of the same nature. It will end up in the same way; there is no way it can avoid that state.'

"Further, the practitioner sees a corpse thrown onto a charnel ground, pecked at by crows, eaten by hawks, vultures, and jackals, and infested with maggots and worms, and they contemplate this truth as regards their own body, 'This body of mine is of the same nature, it will end up in the same way, there is no way it can avoid that state.'

"Further, the practitioner sees a corpse thrown onto a charnel ground; it is just a skeleton with a little flesh and blood sticking to it, and the bones are held together by the ligaments.

"Further, the practitioner sees a corpse thrown onto a charnel ground; it is just a skeleton, no longer adhered to by any flesh, but still smeared by a little blood, the bones still held together by the ligaments.

"Further, the practitioner sees a corpse thrown onto a charnel ground; it is just a skeleton, no longer adhered to by any flesh nor smeared by any blood, but the bones are still held together by the ligaments.

"Further, the practitioner sees a corpse thrown onto a charnel ground; all that is left is a collection of bones scattered here and there; in one place a hand bone, in another a shin bone, a thigh bone, a pelvis, a spinal column, a skull.

"Further, the practitioner sees a corpse thrown onto a charnel ground; all that is left is a collection of bleached bones, the color of shells.

"Further, the practitioner sees a corpse thrown onto a charnel ground; it has been lying there for more than one year and all that is left is a collection of dried bones.

"Further, the practitioner sees a corpse thrown onto a charnel ground; all that is left is the dust which comes from the rotted bones, and they contemplate this truth as regards their own body, 'This body of mine is of the same nature, it will end up in the same way. There is no way it can avoid that state.'

III

"Bhikkhus, how does a practitioner remain established in the contemplation of the feelings in the feelings?

"Whenever the practitioner has a pleasant feeling, they are aware, 'I am experiencing a pleasant feeling.' The practitioner practices like this for all the feelings, whether they are pleasant, painful, or neutral, contemplating when they belong to the body and when they belong to the mind.

IV

"Bhikkhus, how does a practitioner remain established in the contemplation of the mind in the mind?

"When their mind is desiring, the practitioner is aware, 'My mind is desiring.' When their mind is not desiring, they are aware, 'My mind is not desiring.' They are aware in the same way concerning a hating mind, a confused mind, a collected mind, a dispersed mind, an expansive mind, a narrow mind, the highest mind, a concentrated, and liberated mind.

V

"Bhikkhus, how does a practitioner remain established in the contemplation of the objects of mind in the objects of mind?

"First of all, they contemplate the objects of mind in the objects of mind with regard to the Five Hindrances. How do they contemplate this?

"When sensual desire is present in them, they are aware, 'Sensual desire is present.' Or when sensual desire is not present in them, they are aware, 'Sensual desire is not present.' When sensual desire begins to arise, they are aware of it. When sensual desire that has already arisen is abandoned, they are aware of it. When sensual desire has been abandoned and does not arise again, they are aware of it.

"They practice in the same way concerning anger, dullness and drowsiness, agitation and remorse, and doubt.

"Further, the practitioner contemplates the objects of mind in the objects of mind with regard to the five aggregates of clinging. How do they contemplate this?

"They contemplate like this: 'Such is form. Such is the arising of form. Such is the disappearance of form. Such is feeling. Such is the arising of feeling. Such is the disappearance of feeling. Such is perception. Such is the arising of perception. Such is the disappearance of perception. Such are mental formations. Such is the arising of mental formations. Such is the disappearance of mental formations. Such is consciousness. Such is the arising of consciousness. Such is the disappearance of consciousness.

"Further, bhikkhus, the practitioner contemplates the objects of mind in the objects of mind with regard to the six sense organs and the six sense objects. How do they contemplate this?

"They are aware of the eyes and aware of the form, and they are aware of the internal formations which are produced in dependence on these two things. They are aware of the birth of a new internal formation, and are aware of abandoning an already produced internal formation, and are aware when an abandoned internal formation does not arise again.

"They are aware in the same way of the ears and sound, the nose and smell, the tongue and taste, the body and touch, the mind and objects of mind.

"Further, bhikkhus, the practitioner remains established in the contemplation of the objects of mind in the objects of mind with regard to the Seven Factors of Awakening.

"How do they remain established in the practice of contemplation of the Seven Factors of Awakening?

"When the factor of awakening, mindfulness, is present in them, they are aware, 'Mindfulness is present.' When mindfulness is not present in them, they are aware, 'Mindfulness is not present.' They are aware when not-yet-born mindfulness is being born and when already-born mindfulness is perfectly developed.

"In the same way, they are aware of the factors of investigation, diligence, joy, ease, concentration, and equanimity.

"Further, bhikkhus, a practitioner remains established in the contemplation of objects of mind in the objects of mind with regard to the Four Noble Truths.

"How, bhikkhus, does the practitioner remain established in the contemplation of the Four Noble Truths?

"When suffering is present, the practitioner is aware, "This is suffering." When the cause of suffering is present, the practitioner is aware, "This is the cause of suffering." When the end of suffering is present, they are aware, "This is the end of suffering." When the path that leads to the end of suffering is present, they are aware, "This is the path that leads to the end of suffering."

"This is how the practitioner remains established in the contemplation of the body in the body, the feelings in the feelings, the mind in the mind, and the objects of mind in the objects of mind either from within or from without, or both from within and from without in any of these establishments. They remain established in the contemplation of the process of coming-to-be, or the process of dissolution, or the process of coming-to-be and the process of dissolution in each of these establishments. Or they are mindful of the fact, 'There is this establishment of mindfulness here,' until understanding and full awareness come about. They remain established in the contemplation, free, not caught in any worldly consideration. That is how to practice the four establishments of mindfulness in the four establishments of mindfulness, O bhikkhus."

VI

"Bhikkhus, those who practice the Four Establishments of Mindfulness for seven years can expect one of two fruits—the highest understanding in this very life or, if there remains some residue of affliction, they can attain the fruit of no-return.

"Let alone seven years, bhikkhus, whoever practices the Four Establishments of Mindfulness for six, five, four, three, two years or one year, for seven, six, five, four, three, or two months, one month or half a month, can also expect one of two fruits—either the highest understanding in this very life or, if there remains some residue of affliction, they can attain the fruit of no-return.

"That is why I said that this path, the path of the four grounds for the establishment of mindfulness, is the one path, which can help beings realize purification, transcend grief and sorrow, destroy pain and anxiety, travel the right path, and realize nibbana."

The bhikkhus were delighted to hear the teaching of the Buddha. They took it to heart and put it into practice.

Satipaṭṭhāna Sutta, Majjhima Nikāya 10*

* For commentary, see Thich Nhat Hanh, *Transformation and Healing: Sutra on the Four Establishments of Mindfulness*, Revised Edition (Berkeley, CA: Parallax Press, 2006).

Discourse on the Five Ways of Putting an End to Anger

I heard these words of the Buddha one time when he was staying in the Anathapindika Monastery in the Jeta Grove near the town of Shravasti.

One day the Venerable Shariputra said to the monks, "Friends, today I want to share with you five ways of putting an end to anger. Please listen carefully and put into practice what I teach."

The bhikshus agreed and listened carefully.

The Venerable Shariputra then said, "What are these five ways of putting an end to anger?

"My friends, this is the first way. If there is someone whose bodily actions are not kind but whose words are kind, if you feel anger toward that person but you are wise, you will know how to meditate in order to put an end to your anger.

"My friends, say there is a bhikshu practicing asceticism who wears a patchwork robe. One day he is going past a garbage pile filled with excrement, urine, mucus, and many other filthy things, and he sees in the pile one piece of cloth still intact. Using his left hand, he picks up the piece of cloth, and he takes the other end and stretches it out with his right hand. He observes that this piece of cloth is not torn and has not been stained by excrement, urine, sputum, or other kinds of filth. So he folds it and puts it away to take home, wash, and sew into his patchwork robe. My friends, if you are wise, when someone's bodily actions are not kind but his words are kind, you should not pay attention to his unkind bodily actions, but only be attentive to his kind words. This will help you put an end to your anger. Someone who is wise should practice in this way.

"My friends, this is the second method. If you become angry with someone whose words are not kind but whose bodily actions are kind, if you are wise, you will know how to meditate in order to put an end to your anger.

"My friends, say that not far from the village there is a deep lake, and the surface of that lake is covered with algae and grass. There is someone who comes near that lake who is very thirsty, suffering greatly from the heat. They take off their clothes, jump into the water, and using their hands to clear away the algae and grass, enjoy bathing and drinking the cool water of the lake. It is the same, my friends, with someone whose words are not kind but whose bodily actions are kind. Do not pay attention to that person's words. Only be attentive to their bodily actions in order to be able to put an end to your anger. Someone who is wise should practice in this way.

"Here is the third method, my friends. If there is someone whose bodily actions and words are not kind, but who still has a little kindness in their heart, if you feel anger toward that person and are wise, you will know how to meditate to put an end to your anger.

"My friends, say there is someone going to a crossroads. They are weak, thirsty, poor, hot, deprived, and filled with sorrow. When they arrive at the crossroads, they see a buffalo's footprint with a little stagnant rainwater in it. They think, 'There is very little water in this buffalo's footprint. If I use my hand or a leaf to scoop it up, I will stir it up and it will become muddy and undrinkable. Therefore, I will not be able to remove my thirst, deprivation, heat, and sorrow, so I will have to kneel down with my arms and knees on the earth, put my lips right to the water, and drink it directly.' Straightaway, they do just that. My friends, when you see someone whose bodily actions and words are not kind, but where there is still a little kindness in their heart, do not pay attention to their actions and words, but to the little kindness that is in their heart so that you may put an end to your anger. Someone who is wise should practice in this way.

"This is the fourth method, my friends. If there is someone whose words and bodily actions are not kind, and in whose heart there is nothing that can be called kindness, if you are angry with that person and you are wise, you will know how to meditate in order to put an end to your anger.

"My friends, suppose there is someone on a long journey who falls sick. He is alone, completely exhausted, and not near any village. He falls into despair, knowing that he will die before completing his journey. If at that point, someone comes along and sees this man's situation, they immediately take the man's hand and lead him to the next village, where they take care of him, treat his illness, and make sure he has everything he needs by way of clothes, medicine, and food. Because of this compassion and loving kindness, the man's life is saved. Just so, my friends, when you see someone whose words and bodily actions are not kind, and in whose heart there is nothing that can be called kindness, give rise to this thought: 'Someone whose words and bodily actions are not kind and in whose heart is nothing that can be called kindness, is someone who is undergoing great suffering. Unless they meet a good spiritual friend, there will be no chance for them to transform and go to realms of happiness.' Thinking like this, you will be able to open your heart with love and compassion toward that person.

You will be able to put an end to your anger and help that person. Someone who is wise should practice like this.

"My friends, this is the fifth method. If there is someone whose bodily actions are kind, whose words are kind, and whose mind is also kind, if you are angry with that person and you are wise, you will know how to meditate in order to put an end to your anger.

"My friends, suppose that not far from the village there is a very beautiful lake. The water in the lake is clear and sweet, the bed of the lake is even, the banks of the lake are lush with green grass, and all around the lake, beautiful fresh trees give shade. Someone who is thirsty, suffering from heat, whose body is covered in sweat, comes to the lake, takes off their clothes, leaves them on the shore, jumps down into the water, and finds great comfort and enjoyment in drinking and bathing in the pure water. Their heat, thirst, and suffering disappear immediately. In the same way, my friends, when you see someone whose bodily actions are kind, whose words are kind, and whose mind is also kind, give your attention to all their kindness of body, speech, and mind, and do not allow anger or jealousy to overwhelm you. If you do not know how to live happily with someone who is as fresh as that, you cannot be called someone who is wise.

"My dear friends, I have shared with you the five ways of putting an end to anger."

When the bhikshus heard the Venerable Shariputra's words, they were happy to receive them and put them into practice.

Madhyama Āgama 25
(Corresponds with Āghātapaṭivinaya Sutta
[Discourse on Water as an Example], Aṅguttara Nikāya 5.162)

Discourse on the White-Clad Disciple

I heard these words of the Buddha one time when he was staying at the monastery in the Jeta Grove near Shravasti that had been donated by the layman Anathapindika. On that day, Anathapindika came with five hundred other lay students to the hut where Shariputra resided. They bowed their heads in reverence to him and sat down respectfully to one side. Venerable Shariputra offered them skillful teachings, which brought them joy and gave rise in them a longing for the Three Jewels and the practice of the true Dharma. Then, Shariputra and the five hundred lay students went to visit the Buddha. There Shariputra, Anathapindika, and the the lay students prostrated at the Buddha's feet and sat down to one side.

When he observed that everyone was seated, the Buddha addressed Shariputra, saying, "Shariputra, if lay students of the Buddha, those who wear white robes, practice the Five Mindfulness Trainings and attain without hardship the four ways of the mind abiding happily in the here and now, you know they will not fall into the realms of hell, hungry ghosts, animals, and other suffering paths in the future.

"Such practitioners have attained the fruit of stream-enterer. Shariputra, how do lay students of the Buddha, those who wear white robes, practice the Five Mindfulness Trainings and the four ways of the mind abiding happily in the here and now?

"Lay students of the Buddha refrain from killing, put an end to killing, rid themselves of all weapons. They are capable of feeling shame before others and for themselves; they practice love and compassion, and protect all living beings, even the smallest insects. They uproot from within themselves any intention to kill. This is the First Mindfulness Training that the white-clad disciples keep.

"Lay students of the Buddha refrain from taking what has not been given, put an end to taking what has not been given. They find joy in being generous without expecting anything in return. Their minds are not obscured by greed. They constantly guard their own honesty and uproot from within themselves any intention to take what has not been given. This is the Second Mindfulness Training that the white-clad disciples keep.

"Lay students of the Buddha refrain from sexual misconduct, put an end to sexual misconduct, and protect everyone—those under the care of their father, mother, or both father and mother; their elder sister or elder brother; their parents-in-law or other in-laws; those of the same sex; the wife, daughter, husband, or son of another; and those who have been raped, or who have been prostitutes. Lay students of the Buddha uproot from within themselves any intention to commit sexual misconduct. This is the Third Mindfulness Training that the white-clad disciples keep.

"Lay students of the Buddha refrain from saying what is not true, put an end to saying what is not true. They say only what is true, and they find great joy in saying what is true. They always abide in truth and are completely reliable, never deceiving others. They have uprooted from within themselves any intention to say what is not true. This is the Fourth Mindfulness Training that the white-clad disciples keep.

"Lay students of the Buddha refrain from drinking alcohol, put an end to drinking alcohol. They uproot from within themselves the habit of drinking alcohol. This is the Fifth Mindfulness Training that the white-clad disciples keep.

"Shariputra, how do lay students of the Buddha attain the four ways of the mind abiding happily in the here and now with ease and without hardship? They practice recollecting the Buddha. They meditate as follows: The Buddha is fully and rightly awakened, without any attachments; his understanding and practice are perfected; he is the Well-Gone One; the one who knows and fully understands the world; the one who tames humankind, a teacher of humans and gods; the Awakened One; the World-Honored One. When they recollect the Buddha in this way, unwholesome desires come to an end, and in their minds no unwholesome, or impure thoughts, grief or anxiety arise. As a result of contemplating the Buddha, their thoughts are clear, they feel joy, and they arrive at the first of the four ways of the mind abiding happily in the here and now, with ease and without any hardships.

"Shariputra, the lay students of the Buddha practice recollecting the Dharma. They meditate as follows: the Dharma is taught by the Lord Buddha with great skill; it can lead to complete liberation; it can lead to a state of no afflictions; it is cool and refreshing; its value is timeless. When lay students of the Buddha meditate on and observe the Dharma in this way, all unwholesome desires come to an end, and in their minds no unwholesome or impure thoughts, grief or anxiety arise. As a result of contemplating the Dharma, their thoughts are clear, they feel joy, and they arrive at the second of the four ways of the mind abiding happily in the here and now, with ease and without any hardship.

"Shariputra, the lay students of the Buddha practice recollecting the

Sangha, meditating as follows: the noble community of the Tathagata is advancing in a good direction; it is on an upright path; it is oriented toward the Dharma; it lives the teachings in the way they are meant to be lived. In that community, there are the four pairs and the eight grades—realized arhats and those who are realizing the fruit of arhatship, non-returners and those who are realizing the fruit of non-returning, once-returners and those who are realizing the fruit of once-returning, and stream-enterers and those who are realizing the fruit of stream-entry. The noble community of the Tathagata has successfully realized the practice of the mindfulness trainings, the practice of concentration, and the practice of insight. It has liberation and the knowledge of liberation. It is worthy of respect, reverence, being served, and offerings. It is a beautiful field of merit for the world. As a result of contemplating the Sangha, their thoughts are clear, they feel joy, and they arrive at the third of the four ways of the mind abiding happily in the here and now, with ease and without any hardship.

"Shariputra, the lay students of the Buddha practice recollection of the mindfulness trainings, meditating as follows: the mindfulness trainings have no shortcomings, flaws, impurities, and remain refined; and they help us abide in the land of the Tathagata. The mindfulness trainings are not of the nature to deceive. They are always praised, accepted, practiced, and guarded by the holy ones. As a result of contemplating these Trainings, the students' thoughts are clear, they feel joy, and they arrive at the fourth of the four ways of the mind abiding happily in the here and now, with ease and without any hardship.

"Shariputra, remember that white-clad disciples of the Buddha who practice in this way will not descend into hell realms, hungry ghost realms, animal realms, or any other realms of suffering. They have experienced the fruit of stream-entry, and do not fall back into unwholesome states. Having entered the stream, they cannot help but go in the direction of right awakening. They will only need to return to the world of gods or humans seven more times before they arrive at complete liberation from suffering."

Thus spoke the Buddha. The Venerable Shariputra, the monks and nuns, the layman Anathapindika, and the five hundred lay students heard these words and were delighted to put them into practice.

Upāsaka Sūtra, Madhyama Āgama 128*

In consultation with Aṅguttara Nikāya, 5.179

*For commentary, see Thich Nhat Hanh, *For a Future to Be Possible* (Berkeley, CA: Parallax Press, 1998).

Discourse on Measuring and Reflecting

Thus have I heard. On one occasion the Venerable Mahamoggallana was staying with the Bhagga people at Sumsumaragiri, in the Deer Park in the Bhesakala Grove. The Venerable Mahamoggallana addressed the bhikkhus, "My friends."

"Yes, friend," they replied to the Venerable Mahamoggallana.

The Venerable Mahamoggallana spoke as follows:

"My friends, suppose there is a bhikkhu who says to the other bhikkhus: 'Please talk to me, Reverend Bhikkhus. I want you to be kind to me and speak to me.' If he has characteristics that make other people not want to talk to him, if he is impatient, not open, not good at accepting constructive criticism or the words of advice and instruction from friends in the practice, then they will think that they cannot speak to, teach, or have confidence in him. My friends, what are the qualities that make others look on a bhikkhu as someone who is difficult to talk to?

"My friends, a bhikkhu who is attached to wrong desires and is carried away by wrong desires is difficult to talk to.

"These are other reasons that make it difficult to talk to him: if that person praises himself and despises others; he is easily angered and mastered by his anger; because he is angry, he bears a grudge; because he is angry, he is bad-tempered; because he is angry, he speaks in a bad-tempered way; he accuses one who has corrected him; he disparages one who has corrected him; he corrects in turn one who has corrected him; he questions in turn the one who has questioned him; he evades the criticism by posing irrelevant questions; he gives irrelevant answers; he manifests ill-temper, anger, and sulkiness; he does not succeed in explaining his behavior when asked about about his misbehavior; he is uncouth and ill-willed; he is jealous and greedy; he is hypocritical and deceitful; he is stubborn and arrogant; or he is worldly and clings to things that belong to this world and finds it difficult to let go. These, my friends, are the habit energies that isolate a bhikkhu and make it difficult for his friends in the practice to talk to him.

"My friends, suppose there is a bhikkhu who requests of other bhikkhus: 'Please talk to me, Reverend Bhikkhus. I want you to offer me guidance.' If he is easy to talk to, endowed with qualities that make him easy to deal with, patient, tolerant, open, and able to accept constructive criticism or words of advice and instruction from friends in the practice, then those who practice the path of sublime conduct with him will think, 'He is someone we can talk to, someone we can instruct, someone we can have confidence in.' What are the qualities that make someone easy to approach?

"My friends, a bhikkhu who is not caught in wrong desires and is not controlled by wrong desires is easy to approach and talk to. He does not praise himself and despise others; he is not easily angered or mastered by his anger; because he is not angry, he does not bear a grudge; because he is not angry, he is not bad-tempered; because he is not angry, he does not speak in a bad-tempered way; he does not accuse one who has corrected him; he does not disparage one who has corrected him; he does not correct in turn one who has corrected him; he does not evade the criticism by posing irrelevant questions; he does not give irrelevant answers; he does not manifest ill-temper, anger, and sulkiness; he succeeds in explaining his behavior when asked about his misbehavior; he is not jealous and greedy; he is not hypocritical and deceitful; he is not stubborn and arrogant; he is not worldly, nor does he cling to things that belong to this world, and he does not find it difficult to let go. These, my friends, are the qualities that make it easy to approach and talk to him.

"My friends, one should infer one's own state by considering the state of others in the following way: 'That person has wrong desires and is controlled by his wrong desires; therefore, I do not find him easy to approach. If I had wrong desires and were controlled by those wrong desires, others would not find me easy to approach.' When one sees this clearly, one should make the following determination: 'May I not be attached to wrong desires or be controlled by those wrong desires.'

"This method of reflection needs to be practiced in other cases, such as praising oneself and despising others, being easily angered and mastered by anger, and so on.

"My friends, this is how a bhikkhu should reflect on himself: 'At this moment, am I attached to wrong desires and controlled by wrong desires?' If when a bhikkhu reflects in this way, he knows, 'At this moment, I am attached to wrong desires and controlled by wrong desires,' then he should practice diligently to put an end to these unwholesome mental formations. If, on the other hand, when he reflects, he knows, 'At this moment, I am not attached to wrong desires and not controlled by wrong desires,' then a bhikkhu should live with a feeling of happiness, and he should practice diligently to nourish and increase these wholesome mental formations.

"This method of reflection needs to be practiced in other cases, such as praising oneself and despising others, becoming easily angered and mastered by anger, and so on.

"If, my friends, when he reflects, a bhikkhu sees clearly that he has not yet given up all these unbeneficial qualities, then he should practice diligently to give them all up. If, when he reflects, a bhikkhu sees clearly that he has given up all these unwholesome mental formations, then he should live with a feeling of happiness, and he should practice diligently to nourish and increase these wholesome mental formations.

"It is like when a young person who is fond of adorning himself contemplates his face in the mirror or a bowl of clear water. If he sees dirt or a blemish on his face, he tries to clean it. If he does not see dirt or a blemish, he thinks to himself, 'It is good, my face is clean.'

"So, my friends, if a bhikkhu reflects and sees that all these unwholesome mental formations have not yet been given up, then he practices diligently to give them all up. If he sees that he has given them all up, he feels happy about this and knows that he needs to practice diligently in order to nourish and increase these wholesome mental formations."

The Venerable Mahamoggallana had spoken. The Bhikkhus were delighted, and they accepted their teacher's words with full confidence."

Anumāna Sutta, Majjhima Nikāya 15

Discourse on the Teachings to Be Given to the Sick

I heard these words of the Buddha one time when the Lord was staying in the monastery in the Jeta Grove in the Anathapindika monastery, near Shravasti. At that time the householder Anathapindika was seriously ill. When the Venerable Shariputra was told this, he immediately went to Ananda and said, "Brother Ananda, let us go and visit the layman Anathapindika.

The Venerable Ananda put on his robe and, holding his bowl, went into the town of Shravasti with the Venerable Shariputra to make the alms-round. The two of them stopped at every house until they came to the house of the layman Anathapindika and they went in to visit him. After he had sat down, the Venerable Shariputra asked the layman Anathapindika, "How is your illness? Is it getting better or worse? Is the physical pain easing at all or is it getting greater?" The householder Anathapindika replied, "Venerable monks, it does not seem to be getting better. The pain is not easing. It is getting greater all the time." Shariputra said, "Friend Anathapindika, let us now practice together the recollection of the Buddha, the Dharma, and the Sangha. The recollection goes like this:

"The Buddha has gone to Suchness, is fully and truly awakened, has perfected understanding and action, has arrived at true happiness, understands the nature of the world, is unequaled in understanding, has conquered the afflictions of human beings, is a teacher of gods and humans, and is the Awakened One, the one who liberates the world.

"The Dharma is the teaching of love and understanding that the Tathagata has expounded. It is deep and lovely, worthy of the highest respect, and very precious. It is a teaching that cannot be compared to ordinary teachings. It is a path of practice for the noble ones.

"The Sangha is the community of practice, guided by the teachings of the Tathagata. The community is in harmony, and within it all aspects of the practice can be realized. The community is respected and precious. It practices the precepts and realizes concentration, insight, and liberation. The sangha is the highest field of merit in the world.

"Friend Anathapindika, if you recollect the Buddha, the Dharma, and the Sangha in this way, the beneficial effects are beyond measure. Recollecting in this way, you can put an end to the obstacles of wrong deeds and the afflictions. You can harvest a fruit that is as fresh and sweet as the nectar of deathlessness. Anyone practicing an upright way of life who knows how to recollect the Three Jewels will have no chance of falling into the three lower realms but will be reborn as a human or a god.

"Friend Anathapindika, now is the time to practice the meditation on the six sense bases:

"These eyes are not me. I am not caught in these eyes.
"These ears are not me. I am not caught in these ears.
"This nose is not me. I am not caught in this nose.
"This tongue is not me. I am not caught in this tongue.
"This body is not me. I am not caught in this body.
"This mind is not me. I am not caught in this mind.

"Now continue your meditation with the six sense objects:

"These forms are not me. I am not caught in these forms.
"These sounds are not me. I am not caught in these sounds.
"These smells are not me. I am not caught in these smells.
"These tastes are not me. I am not caught in these tastes.
"These contacts with the body are not me. I am not caught in these contacts with the body.
"These thoughts are not me. I am not caught in these thoughts.

"Now continue your meditation on the six sense consciousnesses:

"Sight is not me. I am not caught in sight.
"Hearing is not me. I am not caught in hearing.
"Smelling is not me. I am not caught in smelling.
"Tasting is not me. I am not caught in tasting.
"Somatosensory consciousness is not me. I am not caught in somatosensory consciousness.
"Mind consciousness is not me. I am not caught in mind consciousness.

"Now continue your meditation on the six elements:

"The earth element is not me. I am not caught in the earth element.
"The water element is not me. I am not caught in the water element.
"The fire element is not me. I am not caught in the fire element.
"The air element is not me. I am not caught in the air element.
"The space element is not me. I am not caught in the space element.
"The consciousness element is not me. I am not caught in the consciousness element.

"Now continue your meditation on the five aggregates:

"Form is not me. I am not limited by form.
"Feelings are not me. I am not limited by feelings.
"Perceptions are not me. I am not limited by perceptions.
"Mental formations are not me. I am not limited by mental formations.
"Consciousness is not me. I am not limited by consciousness.

"Now continue your meditation on the three times:

"The past is not me. I am not limited by the past.
"The present is not me. I am not limited by the present.
"The future is not me. I am not limited by the future.

"Friend Anathapindika, everything arises and ceases due to causes and conditions. In reality, the nature of everything is not born and does not die, does not come and does not go. When eyes arise, they arise, but they do not come from anywhere. When eyes cease to be, they cease to be, but they do not go anywhere. Eyes are neither nonexistent before they arise, nor are they existent after they arise. Everything that is comes to be because of a combination of causes and conditions. When the causes and conditions are sufficient, eyes are present. When the causes and conditions are not sufficient, eyes are absent. The same is true of ears, nose, tongue, body, and mind; form, sound, smell, taste, touch, and thought; sight, hearing, smelling, tasting, somatosensory and mind consciousness; the six elements, the five aggregates, and the three times.

"In the five aggregates, there is nothing that we can call 'I,' a 'person,' or a 'lifespan.' Ignorance is the inability to see this truth. Because there is ignorance, there are wrong perceptions of formations. Because there are wrong perceptions of formations, there is wrong consciousness. Because there is wrong consciousness, there is the distinction between the perceiver and the perceived. Because there is the distinction between the perceiver and the perceived, there is the distinction between the six organs and the six objects of sense. Because there is the distinction between the six organs and the six objects of sense, there is contact. Because there is contact, there is feeling. Because there is feeling, there is craving. Because there is craving, there is grasping. Because there is grasping, there is being and then birth, death, and the inexpressible mass of suffering and grief.

"Friend Anathapindika, you have meditated that everything that arises is due to causes and conditions and does not have a separate self. That is called 'the meditation on emptiness.' It is the highest and the most profound meditation."

When he had practiced to this point, the layman Anathapindika began to cry and tears flowed down his cheeks. Venerable Ananda asked him, "Friend, why are you crying? Has your meditation not been successful? Do you have some regret?" The layman Anathapindika replied, "Venerable Ananda, I do not regret anything. The meditation has been most successful. I am crying because I am so deeply moved. I have been fortunate to have been able to serve the Buddha and his community for many years, yet I have never heard a teaching so wonderful and precious as the teaching transmitted by the Venerable Shariputra today."

Then the Venerable Ananda said to the layman Anathapindika, "Do you not know, friend, that the Buddha often gives this teaching to bhikshus and bhikshunis?" The layman Anathapindika replied, "Venerable Ananda, please tell the Buddha that there are also laypeople with the capacity to listen, understand, and put into practice these deep and wonderful teachings."

After listening to and practicing with the two venerable monks, Anathapindika felt free and at ease, and gave rise to the highest mind. The Venerables Shariputra and Ananda bade him farewell and went back to the monastery, and Anathapindika passed away and was born in the thirty-third heaven.

Ekottara Āgama 51. 8
(In consultation with Majjhima Nikāya 143
and Madhyama Āgama 26)

Discourse on Taking Refuge in the Island of Oneself

I heard these words of the Buddha one time when the Lord was staying in the Mango Grove in the cool shade of the mango trees along the bank of the river Bhadra in the land of Magadha. The elders Shariputra and Maudgalyayana had recently passed away. It was the full-moon day of the Upavasatha Ceremony and the precepts were recited.

The Buddha spread out his sitting mat and sat facing the community. After looking out at those gathered, he said, "As I look at our community, I see a large space left by the Venerables Shariputra and Maudgalyayana who have passed into nirvana. In our Sangha, these venerables were the monks who were the most eloquent in giving Dharma talks, encouraging and instructing all the other monks, nuns, and laypeople.

"O monks, people seek two kinds of riches—material riches and the riches of the Dharma. In their search for material riches, they can go to worldly people. In their search for the riches of the Dharma, they could always go to the Venerables Shariputra and Maudgalyayana. The Tathagata is someone who is not searching for anything, whether it is material or the Dharma.

"O monks, do not be sad or anxious because Shariputra and Maudgalyayana have passed into nirvana. On large trees, filled with leaves, sumptuous fruits and flowers, the largest branches also have to break. On jeweled mountains, the highest peaks also have to erode. In the Sangha of the Tathagata, the Venerables Shariputra and Maudgalyayana were the greatest students. So it is natural that these venerables would enter nirvana before you. Do not give rise to feelings of sorrow or anguish.

"All phenomena that are born, exist, and are subject to the influence of other phenomena, in other words, all phenomena that are composite, must abide by the law of impermanence and eventually cease to exist. They cannot exist eternally, without some day being destroyed. I have reminded you many times that everything we cherish and hold dear today, we will have to let go of and be separated from. In not too long a time, I will also pass away. Therefore, I urge you to practice being an island unto yourself, knowing how to take refuge in yourself, and not taking refuge in anyone or anything else.

"Practice taking refuge in the island of the Dharma. Know how to take refuge in the Dharma, and do not take refuge in any other island or person. This means to practice dwelling in the contemplation of the body in the body, using the exercises diligently to nourish right understanding and right mindfulness to master and transform craving and anxiety that belong to the world. Contemplate the body outside the body, using the exercises diligently to nourish right understanding and right mindfulness to master and transform craving and anxiety that belong to the world. That is what is meant by returning to the island of oneself in order to take refuge in the island of oneself. Returning to the island of the right Dharma in order to take refuge in the island of the right Dharma and not taking refuge in any other island or any other thing."

When the bhikshus heard the Buddha offer this teaching, they were all very happy to put it into practice.

Samyukta Āgama 639 (Taisho 99)
In consultation with Samyutta Nikāya 47.14

Discourse on Knowing the Better Way to Catch a Snake

I heard these words one time when the Buddha was staying at the Ana-thapindika Monastery in the Jeta Grove, near Shravasti. At that time, the Bhikshu Arishta, who before being ordained had been a vulture trainer, had the wrong view that according to the teachings of the Buddha, the enjoyment of sense pleasures is not an obstacle to the practice. After hearing this, many bhikshus went to Arishta and asked, "Brother Arishta, is it right that you said that according to your understanding of what the Buddha teaches, the enjoyment of sense pleasures is not an obstacle to the practice?"

Arishta replied, "Yes, friends, it is right. I believe the Buddha does not regard enjoyment of sense pleasures as an obstacle to the practice."

The bhikshus told him, "Brother Arishta, do not speak like that; do not misrepresent and slander the Buddha. The Buddha has never said that. It is not good to misrepresent and slander the Buddha. Brother Arishta, sense pleasures are an obstacle to the practice. The Buddha has used many examples in teaching us this. You should abandon this wrong view." Although the bhikshus counseled Arishta in this way, he did not listen. He still stubbornly held onto his wrong view. He still kept saying that what he thought was the truth and all other views were wrong. After asking him three times to abandon his view to no effect, they stood up and left. They went to the Buddha. They prostrated at his feet, sat to one side and told the Buddha what had happened.

The Buddha summoned Arishta, admonished him, and taught the bhikshus, "Monks, it is important to understand the meaning of my teachings thoroughly and correctly before you teach or put them into practice. If you have not understood the meaning thoroughly and correctly, then ask me or one of those who are wise practitioners of the holy life. There are some people who lack wisdom, and because they perceive the letter or the spirit of the teachings wrongly they take them the opposite way of what was intended, whether the teachings are offered in the form of verse or prose, predictions, verse summaries, interdependent origination, similes, spontaneous utterances, quotations, stories of previous births, wonderful occurrences, detailed commentaries, or clarifications with definitions. These people study to win debates and not to practice to liberate themselves. So, they are caught in the form and not able to receive the true spirit of the teachings. They may go through much hardship, endure difficulties that are not of much benefit, and eventually exhaust themselves.

"They are like someone who tries to catch a poisonous snake in the wild. They see a large snake and immediately reach out their hand to grab it. The snake turns around and bites them on their hand, leg, or some other part of their body. Trying to catch a snake that way has no advantages and only harms them.

"The reason for this is that they do not know the art of catching a snake. Someone who learns the teachings unintelligently is like that. Because they do not know how to study, then they understand the teachings in the wrong way. An intelligent person will know how to receive the words and the spirit of the teachings skillfully and therefore, they will not have distorted views. They do not study with the aim of boasting and debating. They study with the aim of discovering the way of liberation. Therefore they will have no pain or hardship.

"They are like someone who uses a forked stick to catch a snake. When they see a poisonous snake in the wild, they place the stick right below the head of the snake and grab the snake's head with their hand. Even if the snake winds itself around their hand, leg, or another part of their body, it will not bite them. This is the better way to catch a snake, and it will not lead to pain or hardship.

"Bhikshus, a son or daughter of good family who knows how to study the teachings needs to receive the letter and the spirit skillfully without distortion in order to master the Dharma. They do not study with the aim of boasting, debating, or arguing, but only to seek liberation. They do not need to go through hardship and exhaustion.

"Bhikshus, I have taught you the example of the raft many times and told you that you have to let go of it and not hold onto it unnecessarily. For example, a mountain stream overflows and becomes a torrent of floodwater carrying debris. There is someone who wants to cross to the other side but there is no boat or bridge. They think, 'I have work to do on the other side, but I need to find a safe way of crossing.' Thinking like this, they straightaway gather branches and grasses, construct a raft, and use it to cross safely to the other side. Having crossed to the other side, they think, 'I spent a lot of time and energy building this raft, which helped me to reach this shore, so I should not abandon it. Now I will put it on my shoulders or head and carry it with me.' They do just that. Bhikshus, do you think that there is any benefit for that person in doing that?

The bhikshus replied, "No, World-Honored One."

The Buddha said, "How could they have acted so that the raft can continue to give benefit? They could have thought, 'This raft helped me cross the water safely. Now I will release it onto the water or leave it on the riverbank for someone else to use.' Wouldn't that be a more beneficial thing to do?"

The bhikshus replied, "Yes, World-Honored One."

The Buddha taught, "I have given this teaching on the raft many times to remind you how necessary it is to let go of the Dharma, not to mention what is not Dharma.

ॐ

"Bhikshus, there are six bases for views. This means that there are six grounds of wrong perception that we need to drop. What are the six?

"First, there is body. Whether belonging to the past, the future, or the present, whether it is our own body or someone else's, whether subtle or gross, ugly or beautiful, near or far, this body is not mine, is not me, is not the self. Bhikshus, look deeply so that you can see the truth concerning the body.

"Second, there are feelings.

"Third, there are perceptions.

"Fourth, there are mental formations. Whether these phenomena belong to the past, the future, or the present, whether they are our own or someone else's, whether they are subtle or gross, ugly or beautiful, near or far, such phenomena are not mine, are not me, are not the self.

"Fifth, there is consciousness. Whatever we see, hear, know, mentally grasp, observe, or think about at the present time or any other time is not ours, is not us, is not the self.

"Sixth, there is the world. Some people think, 'The world is the self. The self is the world. The world is me. I will continue to exist without changing after I die. I am eternal. I will never perish.' Meditate so you can see that the world is not mine, is not me, is not the self. Meditating like that you will see the truth concerning the world."

ॐ

Upon hearing this, a bhikshu stood up, bared his right shoulder, joined his palms, and asked the Buddha, "World-Honored One, can fear and anxiety arise from an internal source*?"

*"Internal" means coming from the bhikshu himself.

The Buddha replied, "Yes, Suppose someone were to perceive and say, 'In the past this did not exist, then it came into existence but now I cannot grasp it,' they will feel grief, weep, and beat their breast until they lose their mind. This is how fear and anxiety can arise from an internal source."

The bhikshu then asked, "World-Honored One, can fear and anxiety arise from an external source*?"

The Buddha taught, "Yes. Suppose someone were to perceive and say, 'This is myself. This is the universe. The universe is I. I will exist forever.' Then they meet the Buddha or a disciple of the Buddha who has the understanding and intelligence to give them the teachings on letting go of attachment to views of the body, the self, what belongs to the self; teachings on letting go of complexes about the self, internal knots, and the taints. Then they could think, 'This is the end of the world. I have to give up everything. I am not the world. I am not me. I am not the self. I will not exist forever. When I die, I will be completely annihilated. There is nothing to look forward to, to be joyful about, or to remember.' Thinking like this, they will feel grief, weep, and beat their breast until they lose their mind. This is how fear and anxiety can arise from an external source."

ॐ

The Buddha asked, "Bhikshus, do you perceive the five aggregates and the self as permanent, changeless, and not subject to destruction?"

"No, World Honored One."

"Is there anything you can hold onto with attachment that will not cause anxiety, exhaustion, sorrow, suffering, and despair?"

"No, World Honored One."

"Is there any view of self in which you can take refuge that will not cause anxiety, exhaustion, sorrow, suffering, and despair?"

"No, World Honored One."

"Good! Because there is an idea of self, then there is an idea of what belongs to the self. If there is not an idea of self, then there will not be an idea of what belongs to the self. Self and what belongs to the self are two ideas that cannot be grasped and cannot be established. If these wrong perceptions arise in our mind, they will create internal knots. These internal knots arise from ideas that cannot be grasped and cannot be established. Aren't they all wrong perceptions and the result of wrong perceptions in the case of Bhikshu Arishta?"

---

*"External" means coming from someone other than the bhikshu.

༄

The Buddha continued, "If in the case of these six objects (body, feelings, perceptions, mental formations, consciousness, and the world) the bhikshu does not see a self or what belongs to the self, he will not be caught in the bonds of life. Because he is not caught, he has no fear. Having no fear, he realizes nirvana. He knows that the cycle of suffering has come to an end, the holy life has been lived; what needs to be done has been done; there is no birth, no death; and he can perceive things as they are. Such a bhikshu has filled in the moat, crossed the moat, destroyed the enemy citadel, unbolted the door, and is able to look directly into the mirror of noble understanding.

"Bhikshus, that is the Way of the Tathagata and those who have attained liberation. Indra, Prajapati, Brahma, and the other gods in their entourage, however hard they look, cannot find any trace or basis for the consciousness of a tathagata. The Tathagata is a noble fount of freshness and coolness. There is no great heat and no sorrow in this state. When shramanas and brahmans hear me say this, they may slander me, saying that I do not speak the truth, that the monk Gautama proposes a theory of nihilism and teaches absolute nonexistence, while in fact living beings do exist. Bhikshus, the Tathagata has never taught the things they say. In truth, the Tathagata teaches only the ending of suffering in order to attain the state of no-anxiety. If the Tathagata is blamed, criticized, defamed, or beaten, he is not angry, not resentful, and does not want to take revenge. If someone blames, criticizes, defames, or beats the Tathagata, how does he react? The Tathagata thinks, 'It was a past action by the Tathagata that has led to this. If someone respects, honors, or makes offerings to a tathagata, the Tathagata would not on that account feel pleased. He would think only that someone is doing this because the Tathagata has attained the fruit of awakening and transformation.'"

Having heard the Buddha speak thus, the bhikshus, with great joy, put the teachings into practice.

Arișṭa Sūtra, Madhyama Āgama 200
Alagaddūpama Sutta, Majjhima Nikāya 22*

---

*For the complete text and commentary, see Thich Nhat Hanh, *Thundering Silence: Sutra on Knowing the Better Way to Catch a Snake* (Berkeley, CA: Parallax Press, 1993).

Discourse on Youth and Happiness

I heard these words of the Buddha one time when the Lord was staying at the Bamboo Forest Monastery near the town of Rajagriha. At that time there was a bhikshu who, in the very early morning, came to the banks of the river, took off his robe, left it on the bank, and went down to the river to bathe. After bathing, he came out of the river, waited until his body was dry, and then put on his robe. At that time a goddess appeared, whose body, surrounded by light, lit up the entire bank of the river. The goddess said to the bhikshu, "Venerable, you've recently become a monk. Your hair is still black; you are still young. At this time in your life, shouldn't you be perfumed with oils, adorned with gems and fragrant flowers, enjoying the five kinds of sensual desire? Meanwhile, you have abandoned your loved ones and turned your back on the worldly life, practicing celibacy. You have shaved your hair and beard, donned the monk's robe, and placed your faith in monastic practice. Why have you abandoned the pleasures of this moment to seek pleasures in a distant future?"

The bhikshu replied, "I have not abandoned the present moment in order to seek pleasures in a distant future. I have abandoned pleasures that are untimely for the deepest happiness of this moment."

The goddess asked, "What is meant by abandoning pleasures that are untimely for the deepest happiness of this moment?"

And the bhikshu replied, "The World-Honored One has taught: in the untimely joy associated with sensual desire there is little sweetness and much bitterness, tiny benefits, and a great potential to lead to disaster. Now, as I dwell in the Dharma in the here and now, I've given up the burning fire of afflictions. The Dharma can be perceived here and now. It is outside of time and invites us to come and see it directly. It is to be realized and experienced by each of us for ourselves. That is what is called abandoning untimely pleasures in order to realize true happiness in the present moment."

The goddess asked the bhikshu again, "Why does the World-Honored One say that in the untimely pleasure of sensual desire there is little sweetness and much bitterness, its benefit is tiny but its potential to lead to disaster is great? Why does he say that if we dwell in the Dharma that can be perceived here and now we are able to give up the flames of the afflictions that burn us? Why does he say that the Dharma can be perceived in the here and now, is outside of time, invites us to come and see it directly, and is realized and experienced by each of us for ourselves?"

The bhikshu replied, "I have only been ordained for a short time. I do not have the skill to explain to you the teachings and the precepts that the World-Honored One has proclaimed. The Tathagata is staying nearby, in the Bamboo Forest. Why don't you go to him and ask your questions directly? The Tathagata will teach you the Dharma, and you can receive and put it into practice as you wish."

The goddess replied, "Venerable bhikshu, at this moment the Tathagata is surrounded by gods and goddesses with special powers. It would be difficult for me to have the chance to approach him and ask about the Dharma. If you would be willing to ask the Tathagata these questions on my behalf, I will follow you."

The bhikshu replied, "I will help you."

The goddess said, "Venerable, then I will follow you."

The bhikshu went to the place where the Buddha was staying, bowed his head and prostrated before the Buddha, then withdrew a little and sat down to one side. He repeated the conversation he had had with the goddess, and then said, "World-Honored One, if this goddess was sincere, she would be here now. If not, she probably is not here now." At that moment, the voice of the goddess was heard from afar, "Venerable monk, I am here. I am here."

The World-Honored One immediately offered this verse:

> People are caught in desire,
> since they do not understand it clearly.
> The delusion connected with desire
> takes them on a path to death."

The Buddha then asked the goddess, "Do you understand this verse? If not, you may say so."

The goddess addressed the Buddha, "I have not understood, World-Honored One. I have not understood, Well-Gone One."

So the Buddha recited another verse for the goddess:

> "When you know the true nature of desire,
> the mind of desire will not arise.

When the mind of desire does not arise
no one is able to tempt you."

Then Buddha asked the goddess, "Have you understood this verse? If not, you may say so."

The goddess addressed the Buddha: "I have not understood, World-Honored One. I have not understood, Well-Gone One."

So the Buddha recited another verse for the goddess:

"The complexes of inferiority, superiority, and equality
bring about so many difficulties
When these three complexes are overcome,
your mind is no longer disturbed."

Then Buddha asked the goddess, "Have you understood this verse? If not, you may say so."

The goddess addressed the Buddha, "I have not understood, World-Honored One. I have not understood, Well-Gone One."

So the Buddha recited another verse for the goddess:

"Ending desire, overcoming the three complexes,
your mind is stilled, you have nothing to long for.
You lay aside all affliction and sorrow,
in this life and in lives to come."

Then Buddha asked the goddess, "Have you understood this verse? If not, you may say so."

The goddess addressed the Buddha, "I have understood, World-Honored One. I have understood, Well-Gone One."

The Buddha had finished the teaching. The goddess was delighted at what she had heard. Practicing in accord with these teachings, she disappeared. Not a trace of her was to be seen anywhere.

Samiddhi Sutta, Samyukta Āgama 1078 (Taisho 99)
(Corresponds to Samyutta Nikāya 1.20.)

Discourse on the Dharma Seal
(The Three Doors of Liberation)

I heard these words of the Buddha one time when the Lord was residing at Shravasti with his community of bhikshus. One day, he told the community, "Do you know of the wonderful Dharma Seal? Today I would like to tell you about it and explain it to you. Please use your pure mind to listen and receive it with care, and make the best effort to remember and practice it." The community of bhikshus replied, "Wonderful, World-Honored One! Please teach us. We will listen carefully."

The Buddha said, "Emptiness is neither being nor nonbeing. It is free from all wrong views. It is neither produced nor destroyed, and it cannot be grasped by views. Why is this so? Because emptiness cannot be located in space. It has no form. It is not an object of perception. It has never been born, and the intellect cannot grasp it, nor can it be grasped in any other way. Because it cannot be grasped, it embraces all phenomena and dwells only in non-discursive, nondiscriminative wisdom. This is the true and right understanding, bhikshus! You should know that not only emptiness, but all phenomena are like that. This is the Dharma Seal.

"The Dharma Seal is the Three Doors of Liberation. It is the basic teaching of all Buddhas, the eye of all Buddhas, the place all Buddhas go back to. Listen and receive it with care. Memorize it well in order to reflect and meditate right in the heart of reality.

"Bhikshus, find a quiet place to meditate on the true nature of things, such as in a forest under a tree. There you can see that the body is impermanent, subject to change, unstable and empty, and as a result, you will not be attached to form. You will reach the nondiscriminative understanding of form. Then do the same for feelings, perceptions, mental formations, and consciousness. See that they are impermanent, subject to change, unstable, and empty of a separate self, and rise above wrong views about them. Realize the nondiscriminative understanding of feelings, perceptions, mental formations, and consciousness. Bhikshus, the five aggregates are empty. They are produced from the mind. Once the mind stops operating, the aggregates stop operating as well. When you see this, you will be liberated, free from all views. This is emptiness, the First Door of Liberation.

"Bhikshus, dwelling in concentration, meditate on forms as sense objects and you will see their dissolution, and be free from the illusory nature of perception vis-à-vis form. Meditate as such for the other sense objects: sound, smell, taste, touch, and objects of mind. You will see their dissolution and be free from the illusory nature of perceptions vis-à-vis sound, smell, taste, touch, and objects of mind. This meditation is called signlessness, the Second Door of Liberation. Once you have entered this door, your understanding and vision will be pure. Because of this purity of understanding, the three defiling qualities of mind—greed, hatred, and delusion—will be uprooted. With these uprooted, you will dwell in the realm of nondiscursive, nondiscriminative insight. When you are dwelling in this insight, views concerning 'me and mine,' and thus all views, no longer have the bases and the occasions to arise.

"Bhikshus, once you are free from the view 'I am,' you no longer consider what you see, hear, feel, and perceive as realities independent of your own consciousness. Why? Because consciousness arises from causes and conditions. Consciousness and the conditions from which it arises are always changing and are impermanent. Because consciousness is impermanent it cannot be grasped. The consciousness skandha like all other phenomena is empty of a separate self so there is nothing that can be created by it. This meditation is called wishlessness, the Third Door of Liberation. Once you enter this door, you experience fully the true nature of all phenomena, and you no longer cling to any dharma because you have seen the unconditioned nature of all phenomena."

The Buddha told the community of bhikshus, "This is the wonderful seal of the Dharma, the Three Doors of Liberation. If you learn and practice it, you will certainly attain pure insight."

The monks were very happy to hear the teaching of the World-Honored One. They paid respect to him and promised to learn and practice this wonderful teaching.

Taisho 104 in consultation
with Samyukta Āgama 80

Discourse on the Eight Realizations of the Great Beings

Wholeheartedly, day and night, disciples of the Awakened One should recite and meditate on the Eight Realizations discovered by the Great Beings.

The First Realization is the awareness that the world is impermanent. Political regimes are subject to fall. Things composed of the four elements are empty, containing within them the seeds of suffering. Human beings are composed of five aggregates and are without a separate self. They are always in the process of change—constantly being born and constantly dying. They are empty of self and without a separate existence. The mind is the source of all confusion, and the body the forest of all unwholesome actions. Meditating on this, you can be released from the round of birth and death.

The Second Realization is the awareness that more desire brings more suffering. All hardships in daily life arise from greed and desire. Those with little desire and ambition are able to relax, their body and mind free from entanglement.

The Third Realization is the awareness that the human mind is always searching outside itself and never feels fulfilled. This brings about unwholesome activity. Bodhisattvas, on the other hand, know the value of having few desires. They live simply and peacefully, so they can devote themselves to practicing the Way. They regard the realization of perfect understanding to be their only career.

The Fourth Realization is the awareness that indolence is an obstacle to practice. You must practice diligently to transform unwholesome mental states that bind you, and you must conquer the four kinds of Mara in order to free yourself from the prisons of the five aggregates and the three worlds.

The Fifth Realization is the awareness that ignorance is the cause of the endless round of birth and death. Bodhisattvas always listen to and learn from others so their understanding and skillful means can develop, and so they can teach living beings and bring them great joy.

The Sixth Realization is the awareness that poverty creates hatred and anger, which creates a vicious cycle of negative thoughts and actions.

When practicing generosity, bodhisattvas consider everyone—friends and enemies alike—to be equal. They do not condemn anyone's past wrongdoings or hate even those presently causing harm.

The Seventh Realization is the awareness that the five categories of sensual desire—money, sex, fame, overeating, and oversleeping—lead to problems. Although you are in the world, try not to be caught in worldly matters. A monk, for example, has in their possession only three robes and one bowl. They live simply in order to practice the Way. Their precepts keep them free of attachment to worldly things, and they treat everyone equally and with compassion.

The Eighth Realization is the awareness that the fire of birth and death is raging, causing endless suffering everywhere. Take the Great Vow to help all beings, to suffer with all beings, and to guide all beings to the Realm of Great Joy.

These Eight Realizations are the discoveries of great beings, buddhas, and bodhisattvas who have practiced diligently the way of understanding and love. They have sailed the Dharmakaya boat to the shore of nirvana, and have then returned to the ordinary world, free of the five sensual desires, their minds and hearts directed toward the noble way. Using these Eight Realizations, they help all beings recognize the suffering in the world. If disciples of the Buddha recite and meditate on these Eight Realizations, they will put an end to countless misunderstandings and difficulties and progress toward enlightenment, leaving behind the world of birth and death, dwelling forever in peace.

Taisho 779*

* For commenatry, see Thich Nhat Hanh *Two Treasures* (Berkeley, CA: Parallax Press, 2007).

The Ten Great Aspirations of Samantabhadra Bodhisattva (Flower Garland Discourse)

Body, speech, and mind, purified, in oneness,
I bow deeply to touch limitless buddhas
of the past, present, and future
throughout all worlds in the Ten directions.

The power of Samantabhadra's vow
enables me to be present everywhere.
Where there is a buddha, I am there.
As buddhas are countless, so too am I.

In a particle of dust are countless buddhas,
all of them present with their own assembly.
The strength of my faith penetrates deeply
into every atom of all Dharma realms.

I aspire to use the great ocean of sound,
giving rise to words of wonderful effect
that praise the Buddha's oceans of virtues,
in the past, present, and future.

I bring these offerings:
garlands of the most beautiful flowers,
incense, music, perfumes, and parasols,
all to adorn the tathagatas and their lands.

I bring food, robes, and fragrant flowers,
torches, sandalwood, sitting mats,
the finest adornments here in abundance —
an offering to the tathagatas.

Inspired by Samantabhadra's vow,
I bring my heart, wide with deep understanding,
with loving faith in the buddhas of the three times,
as an offering to the tathagatas everywhere.

From beginningless time I have acted unskillfully
with craving, hatred, and ignorance
in actions of body, speech, and mind.
Determined now to begin anew, I repent.

I rejoice in every virtuous action
of anyone, in any direction,
of learners and of those who need learn no more,
of buddhas and bodhisattvas.

All beings who are lamps for the world
and those who have just attained enlightenment,
I beg that you will think lovingly of us,
turning the wheel of the Dharma to help the world.

With sincerity, I make a humble request
of the buddhas and those who are about to enter nirvana:
remain forever in the world,
for the benefit and the welfare of all.

I wish to offer praise, respect, and merit
to invite the buddhas to stay and guide all beings to the other shore.
The wholesome roots of repentance, and rejoicing in others' goodness,
I offer to the path of awakening.

I vow to follow all buddhas in order to continue my studies,
and to train myself in the perfect action of Samantabhadra,
as an offering to the tathagatas of the past,
and to all the buddhas of the present in the ten directions.

All the wishes of the future teachers of gods and men
have already been fulfilled.
I vow to learn from the buddhas of the three times
and realize quickly the great enlightenment.

I vow to use the languages of all living beings
to teach them the Dharma.
Encouraging them to practice the prajnaparamita purely,
so that their bodhicitta never diminishes.

May all beings be released from their unwholesome karma
and the mara realms in the world.
May I through countless lands and ages
be of continuous benefit to all beings,
and accompany them for thousands of eons to come.

This merit is transferred to the Three Jewels,
to their nature and form in the Dharma realms.
The Two Truths are perfectly woven together
into the samadhi seal.

The ocean of merit is measureless.
I vow to transfer it and not hold anything for myself.
If any human, out of discrimination and prejudice,
tries to do harm to the path of liberation,
may their obstacles be fully removed.

In each moment, wisdom envelops the Dharma realms,
welcoming all to the place of non-regression.
Space and living beings are without limit,
the same with afflictions and results of past actions.
These four are fully and truly immeasurable.
So, too, is my offering of merit.

Avataṃsaka Sūtra 40,
Taisho 293

Universal Door Chapter (Discourse on the Lotus of the Wonderful Dharma)

Buddha of ten thousand beautiful aspects,
may I ask you this question:
"Why did they give this bodhisattva
the name Avalokita?"

The World-Honored One, wonderfully adorned,
offered this reply to Akshayamati:
"Because actions founded on her deep aspiration
can respond to the needs of any being in any circumstance.

"Her aspirations as wide as the oceans
were made for countless lifetimes.
She has attended to limitless Buddhas,
her great aspiration purified by mindfulness.

"When anyone hears her name or sees her image,
if they give rise to right mindfulness
they will be able to overcome
the suffering of all the worlds.

"When those with cruel intent
push us into a pit of fire,
as we invoke the strength of Avalokita,
the fire becomes a lotus lake.

"Adrift on the waters of the great ocean,
threatened by monsters of the deep,
as we invoke the strength of Avalokita,
we are saved from the storm waves.

"Standing atop Mount Meru,
if someone should push us down,
as we invoke the strength of Avalokita,
we dwell unharmed like the sun in space.

"Chased by a cruel person
down the diamond mountain,
as we invoke the strength of Avalokita,
not even an eyelash will be in danger.

"Encircled and assaulted by bandits
holding swords to wound and to kill,
as we invoke the strength of Avalokita,
the bandits feel our suffering.

"Persecuted by kings and ministers,
about to be executed,
as we invoke the strength of Avalokita,
sword blades shatter into pieces.

"Imprisoned or bound in iron chains,
with hands and feet placed in a yoke,
as we invoke the strength of Avalokita,
we are released into freedom.

"Poisons, curses, and bewitchings
putting us into danger,
as we invoke the strength of Avalokita,
harmful things return to their source.

"Attacked by a fierce and cruel yaksha,
a poisonous naga, or unkind spirit,
as we invoke the strength of Avalokita,
they will do us no harm.

"With wild animals all around
baring their teeth, tusks, and claws,
as we invoke the strength of Avalokita,
they run far away.

"Confronted with scorpions and poisonous snakes,
breathing fire and poisonous smoke,
as we invoke the strength of Avalokita,
they depart, the air clears.

"Caught beneath lightning, thunder, and clouds,
with hail pouring down in torrents,
as we invoke the strength of Avalokita,
the storm ends, the sunlight appears.

"All living beings caught in distress,
oppressed by immeasurable suffering
are rescued in ten thousand ways
by the wonderful power of her understanding.

"Miraculous power with no shortcoming,
wisdom and skillful means so vast —
in the ten directions of all the worlds,
there is no place she does not appear.

"The paths to realms of suffering,
the pain of birth, old age, sickness, and death,
hells, hungry spirits, or animals
are gradually purified.

"Look of truth, look of purity,
look of boundless understanding,
look of love, look of compassion —
the look to be always honored and practiced.

"Look of immaculate light and purity,
the sun of wisdom destroying darkness,
master of fire, wind, and disaster
illuminating the whole world.

"Heart of compassion like rolling thunder,
heart of love like gentle clouds,
water of Dharma nectar raining upon us,
extinguishing the fire of afflictions.

"In the courtroom, the place of lawsuits,
on the fields in the midst of war,
as we invoke the strength of Avalokita,
our enemies become our friends.

"Sound of wonder, sublime sound,
sound of one looking deeply into the world,
sound of the rising tide, the sound that surpasses worldly sounds,
the sound of which we should always be mindful.

"With mindfulness, free from doubts,
when facing catastrophe and death,
Avalokita is the pure and holy one
in whom we need to take refuge.

"We bow in gratitude to the one
who has all the virtues,
regarding the world with compassionate eyes,
an ocean of merit beyond measure."

Saddharmapuṇḍarīka Sūtra, Chapter 25,
Taisho 262*

*For commentary on the Lotus Sutra, see Thich Nhat Hanh, *Peaceful Action, Open Heart* (Berkeley, CA: Parallax Press, 2008).

Store of Precious Virtues Verses:
Prajnaparamita Sutra in Eight Thousand Lines

Bodhisattvas, who, for the sake of the world
remove obstacles and afflictions,
giving rise to a mind confident in nirvana,
rely on the insight that brings us to the other shore.

All the rivers on Roseapple Island,
producing the healing herbs, fresh fruits and flowers,
derive their power from the Naga king
who dwells in the cool Manasarovara Lake.

When hearer-disciples of the Buddha
use skillful means to teach the Dharma and bring beings
    to the other shore,
help people experience joy, taste the fruit of happiness,
and practice the holy life,
it is due to the sacred power of the Tathagata.

The Buddha transmits the Eyes of the Dharma.
His disciples, training according to it,
practice, realize, and teach it to others.
All that is due to the power and strength of the Buddha.

The insight that brings us to the other shore is not to be grasped.
It cannot be attained. There is no enlightenment.
Someone who hears this without feeling terror
is a bodhisattva who has the capacity to understand the Buddha.

Form, feelings, perceptions, mental formations,
and consciousness are empty.
Bodhisattvas are not the least bit caught in anything.
They do not abide in any object of mind
and realize the enlightenment that is not to be grasped.

If bodhisattvas as monastics seek understanding,
they shine light on the five aggregates,
and see their signless nature.
Knowing this, they do not seek the peace of nirvana.
Only then is it the real practice and understanding of a bodhisattva.

What is the object realized by this understanding?
It is to shine the light of insight and see that all is empty.
With this insight, there is no longer any terror.
The bodhisattvas awaken themselves and awaken others.

When practicing, bodhisattvas have to understand the true nature
of body, feelings, perceptions, mental formations, and consciousness.
They shine light on the aggregates and see they are empty
and practice signlessness, not caught in words.

The five aggregates are empty.
The non-practice is called the signless practice.
When you think you are practicing, you do not have the surpassing
    insight,
and the concentration on the signless and nirvana.

If you can practice this silent awakening,
all the buddhas of the past recognize you.
You know the true nature of causes and conditions.
Neither suffering nor delight can touch you.

If you practice and do not see an object of your practice,
you practice in accord with the wisdom of the Sugata.
If you practice with the spirit of non-practice,
this is the insight that brings us to the other shore.

The practice without object cannot be grasped.
Foolish people are caught in the signs "being" and "nonbeing."
Neither being nor nonbeing are the truth.
The bodhisattvas understand this fully and are free.

The Bodhisattvas, knowing that the five aggregates are a magic show,
are free of signs.

Their practice is silent awakening,
which is the practice of the insight that brings us to the other shore.

Advised by good teachers and spiritual friends,
when they hear the Mother of Buddhas' Verses,
they are not afraid.
Taken on the wrong path by false teachers and friends,
they are like a clay pot that has not been fired.

Whom do we call a bodhisattva?
Those who are no longer caught by sensual desire,
They aspire to the fruit of awakening
without being caught by it and are called bodhisattvas.

Whom do we call a mahasattva?
Those who have realized the ultimate truth
and cut through all wrong views in the world.
They are called mahasattvas.

With great generosity, great wisdom, and great authority
they sit aboard the highest vehicle; the vehicle of the Buddha
and give rise to the awakened mind to save all beings.
Thus they are called mahasattvas.

As when a magician at the crossroads,
conjures up an illusory crowd and cuts off their heads,
all worlds are such an illusion.
Knowing this, bodhisattvas feel no fear.

The five aggregates are ropes that bind.
Knowing they are not real, there is no need to untie them.
You practice with the awakened mind of nonattachment.
This is called the highest bodhisattva.

Whom do we call a bodhisattva? —
the one who rides on the great vehicle to bring all beings to the other shore.
The nature and sign of the Great Vehicle are like space.
The joy of the bodhisattvas is calm and steady.

The great vehicle cannot be grasped,
It goes to nirvana wherever it goes.
We cannot recognize the destination. It is like a fire gone out.
That is why it is called "nirvana."

The object of the bodhisattva's practice cannot be grasped.
All three times are purified.
Pure, fearless, and beyond speculation,
This the practice of the insight that brings us to the other shore.

When bodhisattvas engage in the practice of great understanding
and give rise to great love and compassion to bring beings to the other
    shore,
never do they think in terms of "living beings."
This is the practice of the insight that brings us to the other shore.

When bodhisattvas give rise to the notion "living beings"
and practice austerities, caught in the sign "suffering,"
they are caught in the signs "self" and "living being."
This is the practice of the insight that brings us to the other shore.

They know clearly their own nature and that of living beings,
as well as the nature of all objects of mind;
that birth and death are not in opposition.
This is the practice of the insight that brings us to the other shore.

Abandoning all names and words,
abandoning all things that are born and die in the world,
they realize the incomparable understanding of deathlessness.
This is the practice of the insight that brings us to the other shore.

When the bodhisattvas have this as object of their practice,
and know clearly it is a skillful means, and do not pursue anything,
then they know that the nature of this practice is not real.
This is the practice of the insight that brings us to the other shore.

If they are not caught in form, feelings, perceptions,
mental formations, and consciousness,
and only dwell in the right Dharma,
this is the practice of the insight that brings us to the other shore.

Permanent and impermanent, suffering and joy,
self and no-self, all are empty.
They do not abide in the conditioned or the unconditioned.
Like the Buddha, they abide in the practice of signlessness.

If you aspire to attain the fruit of a hearer-disciple,
or self-enlightened buddha, or seek the fruit of buddhahood;
if you do not have perseverance, you cannot arrive.
It is like crossing a great river; you cannot see the other shore.

If you hear these teachings and are determined to apply them
to realize the right and stable awakening, enlightenment,
and see that the nature of all things is your own nature,
that is the great wisdom the Tathagata is describing.

Bodhisattvas who practice great wisdom this way
do not train in the way of a hearer or a self-awakened buddha.
They train only in the boundless knowledge of the Tathagata.
True training is the training of no-training.

They train without being caught in the body, in increase or decrease—
They do not train in any other way.
Their only joy is to train according to the insight into all things.
The same is true of feelings, perceptions, mental formations,
    and consciousness.

Form is neither wisdom nor the absence of wisdom.
Feelings, perceptions, mental formations, and consciousness
    are also like that.
The nature of form is like empty space—
equal, nondual, and undifferentiated.

The basic nature of wrong perception is without limits,
as is the basic nature of all living beings.
The nature of space is the same,
so is the wisdom of the one who understands the world.

The Buddha has said that insight is not form.
Those who are not caught in perceptions realize nirvana.

If someone is not caught in perceptions,
their mind and speech dwell in suchness.

For as many lifetimes as there are grains of sand in the Ganges,
they do not hear the Buddha utter the words "living beings."
Living beings are birthless and pure, from the very beginning.
This is the practice of the insight that brings us to the other shore.

Since every word I have ever uttered
contains the meaning of the insight that brings us to the other shore,
the last Buddha transmitted to me the prediction
that I would be a buddha in a future life.

If someone continues to always receive this insight,
their practice is not any different than that of the Buddha.
Swords, poison, fire, and water, and all the kinds of Mara
will not touch them.

Aṣṭsahāsrakaprajñāpāramitā-Ratnaguṇasaṃcayagāthā,
Taisho 229

The Diamond That Cuts through Illusion

This is what I heard one time when the Buddha was staying in the Anatha-pindika monastery in the Jeta Grove near Shravasti with a community of many, many bodhisattvas including 1,250 fully ordained monks and nuns.

That day, when it was time to make the almsround, the Buddha put on his sanghati robe and, holding his bowl, went into the town of Shravasti to beg for alms, going from house to house. When the almsround was completed, he returned to the monastery to eat the midday meal. Then he put away his sanghati robe and his bowl, washed his feet, arranged his cushion, and sat down.

At that time, the Venerable Subhuti stood up, bared his right shoulder, put his knee on the ground, and, joining his palms respectfully, said to the Buddha, "World-Honored One, it is rare to find someone like you. You always support and place confidence in the bodhisattvas.

"World-Honored One, if sons and daughters of good families want to give rise to the highest, most fulfilled, awakened mind, what should they rely on and what should they do to master their mind?"

The Buddha said to Subhuti, "The bodhisattva-mahasattvas master their mind by meditating as follows: 'However many species of living beings there are—whether born from eggs, from the womb, from moisture, or spontaneously; whether they have form or do not have form; whether they have perceptions or do not have perceptions; or whether it cannot be said of them that they have perceptions or that they do not have perceptions, we must lead all these beings to nirvana so that they can be liberated. Yet when this innumerable, immeasurable, infinite number of beings has become liberated, we do not, in truth, think that a single being has been liberated.'

"Why is this so? If, Subhuti, a bodhisattva still has the notion that a self, a person, a living being, or a life span exists, that person is not a true bodhisattva.

"Moreover, Subhuti, when bodhisattvas practice generosity, they do not rely on any object—any form, sound, smell, taste, touch, or object of mind to practice generosity. That, Subhuti, is the spirit in which bodhisattvas practice generosity, not relying on signs. Why? If bodhisattvas practice generosity without relying on signs, the happiness that results cannot be conceived of. Subhuti, do you think that the space in the eastern quarter can be conceived of or measured?"

"No, World-Honored One."

"Subhuti, can space in the western, southern, or northern quarters, above or below be conceived of or measured?"

"No, World-Honored One."

"Subhuti, if bodhisattvas do not rely on any concept while practicing generosity, the happiness that results from that virtuous act is like space. It cannot be conceived of or measured. Subhuti, the bodhisattvas should let their minds dwell in the teachings I have just given.

"What do you think, Subhuti? Is it possible to recognize the Tathagata by means of bodily signs?"

"No, World-Honored One. When the Tathagata speaks of bodily signs, there are no signs being talked about."

The Buddha said to Subhuti, "In a place where there are signs, in that place there is deception. If you can see the signless nature of signs, you can see the Tathagata."

The Venerable Subhuti said to the Buddha, "In times to come, will there be people who, when they hear these teachings, have real faith in them?"

The Buddha replied, "Do not speak that way, Subhuti. Five hundred years after the Tathagata has passed away, there will still be people who appreciate the joy and happiness that come from observing the precepts. When such people hear these words, they will have faith that this is the truth. Know that such people have sown wholesome seeds not only during the lifetime of one buddha, or even two, three, four, or five buddhas, but have, in fact, planted wholesome seeds during the lifetimes of tens of thousands of buddhas. Anyone who, for even a moment, gives rise to a pure and clear confidence upon hearing these words of the Tathagata, the Tathagata sees and knows that person, and they will attain immeasurable merit because of this understanding. Why?

"Because that person is not caught in the idea of a self, a person, a living being, or a life span, they are not caught in the idea of the Dharma or the non-Dharma; a sign or no-sign. Why? If you are caught in the idea of the Dharma, you are also caught in the ideas of a self, a person, a living being, and a life span. If you are caught in the idea that something is not the Dharma, you are still caught in the ideas of a self, a person, a living being, and a life span. That is why you should not get caught in the idea that this is the Dharma or that is not the Dharma. This is the hidden meaning when the Tathagata says, 'Bhikshus, you should know that the Dharma that I teach is like a raft.' You should let go of the Dharma, let alone what is not the Dharma."

The Buddha asked Subhuti, "In ancient times when the Tathagata practiced under the guidance of the Buddha Dipankara, did the Tathagata attain anything?"

Subhuti answered, "No, World-Honored One. In ancient times when the Tathagata practiced under the guidance of the Buddha Dipankara, he did not attain anything."

"What do you think, Subhuti? Does a bodhisattva adorn a buddha field?"

"No, World-Honored One. Why? To adorn a buddha field is not in fact to adorn a buddha field. That is why it is called adorning a buddha field."

The Buddha said, "So, Subhuti, all the bodhisattva-mahasattvas should give rise to a pure and clear mind in this spirit. When they give rise to this mind, they should not rely on form, sound, smell, taste, touch, or object of mind. They should give rise to an intention with their minds not dwelling anywhere."

"So, Subhuti, when bodhisattvas give rise to the unequaled mind of awakening, they should let go of all ideas. They should not rely on form when they give rise to that mind, nor on sound, smell, taste, touch, or object of mind. They should only give rise to the mind that does not rely on anything.

"The Tathagata has said that all notions are not notions and that all living beings are not living beings. Subhuti, the Tathagata is one who speaks of things as they are, speaks what is true, and speaks in accord with reality. He does not speak falsely. He only speaks in this way. Subhuti, if we say that the Tathagata has realized a teaching, that teaching is neither true nor false.

"Subhuti, bodhisattvas who still depend on notions to practice generosity are like someone walking in the dark. They do not see anything. But when bodhisattvas do not depend on any object of mind to practice generosity, they are like someone with good eyesight walking under the light of the sun. They can see all shapes and colors.

"Subhuti, do not say that the Tathagata has the idea, 'I will bring living beings to the shore of liberation.' Do not think that way, Subhuti. Why? In truth there is no living being for the Tathagata to bring to the other shore. If the Tathagata were to think there was, he would be caught in the idea of a self, a person, a living being, or a life span. Subhuti, what the Tathagata calls a self, essentially is not a self in the way that ordinary people say there is a self. Subhuti, the Tathagata does not consider those ordinary people as ordinary people. That is why he can call them ordinary people.

"What do you think, Subhuti? Can someone visualize the Tathagata by means of the thirty-two marks?"

Subhuti said, "Yes, World-Honored One. We should use the thirty-two marks to visualize the Tathagata."

The Buddha said, "If you say that you can use the thirty-two marks to visualize the Tathagata, then is the Cakravartin also a tathagata?"

Subhuti said, "World-Honored One, I understand your teaching. One should not use the thirty-two marks to visualize the Tathagata."

Then the World-Honored One spoke this verse:

"Someone who looks for me in form
or seeks me in sound
is on a mistaken path
and cannot see the Tathagata."

"Subhuti, if you think that the Tathagata realizes the highest, most fulfilled, awakened mind and does not need to use all the signs, you are wrong. Subhuti, do not think in that way. Do not think that when one gives rise to the highest, most fulfilled, awakened mind, one needs to see all objects of mind as nonexistent, cut off from life. Do not think in that way. One who gives rise to the highest, most fulfilled, awakened mind does not say that all objects of mind are nonexistent and cut off from life."

After they heard the Lord Buddha deliver this discourse, the Venerable Subhuti, the bhikshus and bhikshunis, laymen and laywomen, and gods and asuras, filled with joy and confidence, began to put these teachings into practice.

Vajracchedakaprajñāpāramitā Sutra,
Taisho 335*

*For the complete text and commentary, see Thich Nhat Hanh, *The Diamond That Cuts through Illusion* (Berkeley, CA: Parallax Press, 1992).

Discourse on the Land of Great Happiness

This is what I heard the Buddha say one time when he was staying in the Anathapindika Monastery in the Jeta Grove. At that time the Buddha had with him a sangha of 1,250 bhikshus, all arhats and the most well-known among his senior disciples, including Shariputra, Mahamaudgalyayana, Mahakashyapa, Mahakatyayana, Mahakaushthila, Revata, Shuddhipan-thaka, Nanda, Ananda, Rahula, Gavampati, Pindolabharadvaja, Kaloda-yin, Mahakapphina, Vakkula, and Anuruddha. There were also present bodhisattvas of great stature like Manjushri, Ajita, Gandhahastin, Nityo-dyukta and many other great bodhisattvas as well as countless heavenly beings including Indra.

Then the Buddha addressed Shariputra: "From here hundreds of thou-sands of millions of Buddha worlds to the west, there is a world called Sukhavati (Great Happiness). In that world there is a Buddha whose name is Amita and who is at this very moment teaching the Dharma.

"Shariputra, why is that land called Great Happiness? Because the peo-ple who live there do not know what suffering is. They only enjoy every kind of peace and happiness. And that is why that world is called Great Happiness.

"Shariputra, around Sukhavati there are seven rows of railings, seven rows of spread-out netting and seven rows of trees. All are made of the four kinds of precious jewels. That is why the land is called Great Happiness.

"Furthermore Shariputra, in the land of Great Happiness there are many lakes of the seven precious stones, full of the water of the Eight Virtues. The bed of the lake is made wholly of pure golden sand and on the shores are paths of gold, silver, and crystal. Above these paths are countless pavilions which are built of and decorated with gold, silver, crystal, mother-of-pearl, red agate, and carnelians. The lotus flowers in these lakes are as large as cartwheels. The blue lotuses give out a halo of blue light, the golden lo-tuses a halo of golden light, the pink lotuses a halo of pink light and the white lotuses a halo of white light. The fragrance of the lotuses is subtle, wonderful, and pure.

"Shariputra, Sukhavati is adorned with such beauties as these.

"Furthermore Shariputra, in this Buddha Land people can always hear the sound of heavenly music. The earth is made of pure gold. Six times a day, mandarava flowers rain down from the sky. In the morning the people of this land usually bring baskets to fill them with these wonderful flowers in order to make offerings to the buddhas who live in countless other buddha lands. When it is time for the midday meal, everyone returns to Sukhavati and after eating does walking meditation. Shariputra, that is how extraordinarily beautiful Sukhavati is.

"Furthermore Shariputra, in Sukhavati you can always see different species of birds of many wonderful colors, like white cranes, peacocks, orioles, egrets, kavalinkara, and jivanjiva birds. These birds sing with harmonious, sweet sounds six times a day. In the song of the birds people can hear teachings on different Dharma doors such as the Five Faculties, the Five Powers, the Seven Factors of Awakening, and the Noble Eightfold Path. When the people of this land hear these Dharma sounds, they concentrate their minds and come back to the practice of recollecting Buddha, Dharma, and Sangha.

"Shariputra, do not think that the birds in Sukhavati have been born as the result of past actions. Why? Because the three lower realms of hells, hungry ghosts, and animals do not exist in the land of Amita Buddha. Shariputra, in this land the names of the lower realms do not even exist, how much less their actuality! These birds are manifestations of the Buddha Amita so that the Dharma can be proclaimed widely in his land.

"Shariputra, in this Buddha Land, whenever a light breeze moves the rows of trees and the jeweled netting, people hear a wonderful sound as if a hundred thousand musical instruments are being played together at the same time. When the people hear this sound, they all concentrate their mind on the recollection of the Buddha, the Dharma, and the Sangha. Shariputra, that is how beautiful Sukhavati is.

"Shariputra, why do you think this Buddha is called Amitabha (Limitless Light)? Because he is infinite light which is able to illuminate all worlds in the ten directions and this light and radiance never comes to an end. That is why he is called Amitabha.

"What is more, Shariputra, the life span of this Buddha as well as the life span of everyone who lives in his Buddha Land is limitless. It lasts for innumerable kalpas, that is why he is called Amitayus.

"Shariputra, from the time when Amita Buddha realized enlightenment until now can be reckoned as ten kalpas. Moreover Shariputra, the number of his hearer disciples who have attained the fruit of arhatship is also limitless. It is not possible to calculate them, so great is their number. The number of bodhisattvas in that land is also limitless.

"Shariputra, the land of Amita is made of such virtues as these.

"Shariputra, everyone who is born in Sukhavati naturally has the capacity of non-regression. Among the people living there, many will attain Buddhahood in one more lifetime. The number of these bodhisattvas is infinite, and there is no method of calculation to number them. It may only be expressed by the term limitless.

"Shariputra, when living beings everywhere hear Sukhavati spoken about, they should give rise to the aspiration to be born in this land. Why? Because having been born in this land they will be able to live with and be very close to so many noble practitioners.

"Shariputra, those who lack merit and wholesome roots have little hope of being born in this land. Therefore, Shariputra, if men or women of good families wish to be born in this land, when they hear the name of Amita Buddha, they should recollect that name and wholeheartedly practice contemplation with a mind that is one-pointed and not dispersed for one, two, three, four, five, six, or seven days. When that person passes from this life, they will see Amita Buddha and the holy ones of that land right before their eyes. At the time of their passing, their mind will abide in meditative concentration and will not be deluded or dispersed. That is why they can be born in the Land of Great Happiness.

"Shariputra, it is because I have seen the enormous benefit of this practice that I want to tell all who are listening now to give rise to the aspiration to be born in this land.

"Shariputra, as I am now commending the inestimably great benefits and virtues of Buddha Amita, there are in the east, in the south, in the west, in the north, above and below, buddhas as numberless as the sands of the Ganges, each one seated in their own buddha field, each one with the long tongue of a buddha which is able to embrace the three chiliocosms, announcing with all sincerity, 'Living beings in all worlds, you should have confidence in this sutra, which all the buddhas in the entire cosmos wholeheartedly commend, protect, and keep in mind.'

"Shariputra, why do you think this sutra is wholeheartedly commended, protected, and kept in mind by all buddhas? The reason is that when sons or daughters of good families hear this sutra or hear the name of the Buddha Amita and wholeheartedly practice recollecting the Buddha, they will be protected by all the buddhas, and they will attain the highest fruit of awakening from which they will never regress. So you should have faith in what I am saying and in what all other buddhas are also saying.

"Shariputra, someone who has already given rise, or is now giving rise, or will give rise to the aspiration to be born in Buddha Amita's land, right at the moment when they make this aspiration they realize the highest awakening from which they will never regress. They are already present in that buddha field. It is not necessary that they have been born or are being born or will be born there in order to be present within the Buddha Field of Amita.

"Shariputra, while I am praising the unimaginably great qualities of the buddhas, the buddhas are also praising my unimaginably great qualities saying, 'Buddha Shakyamuni is very rare. In the saha world which is full of the five impurities—the cloudiness of time, the cloudiness of views, the cloudiness of the afflictions, the cloudiness of the idea of living being and life span—he is able to realize the fruit of the highest awakening and is able to teach living beings Dharma doors, which people wherever they are, when they first hear them will find them difficult to believe.

"Shariputra, you should understand that it is something extremely difficult while dwelling in this world which is full of the five kinds of impurity, to realize the fruit of the highest awakening and also to describe to all beings Dharma doors that are as difficult to believe in as this one."

When Shariputra as well as all the bhikshus, heavenly beings, bodhisattvas, warrior gods, and others heard the Buddha deliver this sutra, they all had faith in it, joyously accepted the teaching, and paid respect to the Buddha before returning to their dwelling places.

Sukhavatīvyūha Sūtra,
Taisho 366*

*For commentary see Thich Nhat Hanh, *Finding Our True Home* (Berkeley, CA: Parallax Press, 2003).

Discourse on Emptiness in the True Sense of the Word

This is what I heard one time when the Buddha was residing with the Kuru people, in the village of Kalmasadamya. The World-Honored One addressed the monks: "Now I want to tell you about a teaching, the meaning and the taste of which can be considered as lovely in the beginning, lovely in the middle, and lovely at the end. It is a teaching that is consistent and pure. It can help you to practice the pure and holy life of a monk. Please listen and reflect skillfully on it.

"What is meant by: 'the teaching on emptiness in the true sense of the word?' When the eye arises, it does not come from anywhere, and when it disintegrates it does not go anywhere. Therefore, the eye does not arise as a real entity, and once it has arisen, it has to disintegrate. There is action and the result of action, but there is no actor. When an aggregate disintegrates it is replaced by another. When you look deeply you see that all objects of mind are mere designation. The same is true of the ear, the nose, the tongue, the body, and the mind—they are also not real entities but only mere designation.

"What does mere designation mean? It means that 'Because this is, that is, and because this is born, that is born. Because of ignorance there are formations, because of formations there is consciousness, and so on until there is the entire mass of suffering.' Mere designation also means: 'Because this is not, that is not; because this has ceased, that does not arise anymore. When ignorance ceases, formations cease; when formations cease, consciousness ceases, and so on until this entire mass of suffering ceases.' O monks, that is called emptiness in the true sense of the word."

When the Buddha had spoken, the monks were delighted and joyfully put the teaching into practice.

Samyukta Āgama, 335

Discourse on the Absolute Truth

1. Someone who still abides by a dogmatic view, considering it as the highest in the world, thinking "this is the most excellent" and disparaging other views as inferior, is still considered not to be free from disputes.

2. When seeing, hearing, or sensing something and considering it as the only thing that can bring comfort and advantage to oneself and one's community, you are always inclined to get caught in it and rule out everything else as inferior.

3. Caught in your own view and considering all other views as inferior—this attitude is considered by the wise as bondage, as the absence of freedom. A true practitioner is never too quick to believe what is seen, heard, and sensed, including rules and rites.

4. A true practitioner has no need to set up a new theory for the world, using the knowledge they have picked up or the rules and rites they are practicing. They do not consider themselves as "superior," "inferior," or "equal" to anyone.

5. A true practitioner abandons the notion of self and the tendency to cling to views. They are free and do not depend on anything, even on knowledge. They do not take sides in controversies and do not hold on to any view or dogma.

6. They do not seek for anything or cling to anything, either this extreme or the other extreme, either in this world or in the other world. They have abandoned all views and no longer have the need to seek for comfort or refuge in any theory or ideology.

7. To the wise person, there are no longer any views concerning what is seen, heard, or sensed. How could one judge or have an opinion concerning such a pure practitioner who has let go of all views?

8. Such a practitioner no longer feels the need for setting up dogmas or choosing an ideology. All dogmas and ideologies have been abandoned by such a person. A real noble one is never caught in rules or rites. They are advancing steadfastly to the shore of liberation and will never return to the realm of bondage.

Paramaṭṭhaka Sutta
Sutta Nipāta 4.5

Discourse on Transforming Violence and Fear

1) Let us listen and observe to understand how, from a happy and wholesome state, people have brought society into a state of terror and violence. How have past generations acted for the situation to become like this? I want to talk to you about this suffering and tell you how I have been able to let go of fear.

2) People in the world experience one suffering after another like a fish living in a pond that is drying up day by day. In a situation of suffering, violent thoughts easily arise, and out of ignorance, people seek to relieve their suffering by terrorizing and punishing others.

3) The whole world is burning with violence. Every place is in turmoil. Nowhere is completely safe. Everyone thinks they are better than others and few people know how to let go of their attachments. Unable to see the cause of their suffering, people continue to hold on to their wrong perceptions.

4) People bind themselves up in these wrong perceptions just bringing more ignorance and pain into their lives. I have looked deeply into the minds of those who are not happy, and I have seen hidden under their suffering a sharp-pointed knife. Because they cannot see the sharp-pointed knife hidden in their mind, they are not able to bear the pain.

5) The pain brought about by the sharp-pointed knife lasts a long time without changing. People hold on to that knife wherever they go, so that their pain spills out into the world. Only when they have a chance to recognize the knife and take it out of their hearts, will their suffering cease, and they will have a chance to stop running.

6) Do not allow any worldly fetter to bind you. The roots of wrongdoing and agitation have to be abandoned. Let go of them and do not take refuge in them. If you can put aside wrong desire, you can overcome every misfortune. The practitioner must break free from the cycle of suffering in order to realize their career of liberation.

7) To be a true practitioner you must be wholehearted and sincere, not doing anything based on wrong perception. Go straight on your path, not employing divisive speech. Know how to put out the flames of hatred and break the blocks of wrong desire. If you are able to untie the bonds of the afflictions, you will begin to see the shore of liberation.

8) Let go of pride, do not oversleep, nor sink into a state of torpor. Live and work with moderation, and do not be carried away by the emotions of the majority. Do not be caught by dazzling appearances and know how to turn your back on them. Meditate frequently on the empty nature of all things in order to realize the silence of nirvana.

9) Do not insult anyone. Do not be attracted and caught by deceptive outer appearances. Do not launch into all kinds of amusements, forgetting that the aim of your practice is to relieve suffering in yourself and others.

10) Do not reminisce about what happened in the past and do not have wrong thinking about what will happen. Recognize what is happening in the present moment and do not be carried away by it. In this way, you can walk alone anywhere in the world of the five continents and the four oceans and no one will be jealous of you.

11) I maintain that craving pleasure is the most destructive force. It is the flood that engulfs the whole world. If you can see that, you can master all doubts. You need to apply your mind to the meditation on conditioned co-arising. You should see that if you cannot overcome the defilement of sensual desire it will be difficult to put an end to suffering.

12) Throughout the ages, the number of people who have had the energy to let go of desire for pleasure is very small. However, once you, the practitioner, have let go of desire, you do not feel you have lost anything and you do not need to find another place to go to. The flood subsides all by itself, and nothing can bind you anymore.

13) Relying on the power of the vehicle of insight, the muni crosses to the other shore. Thanks to this insight they have no more anxiety and see they are protected. Birth, death, disasters, and jealousy cannot assail them anymore. By the power of right diligence they realize true peace.

14) When there are no more false notions, your suffering ends. Practitioners meditate on the emptiness of all phenomena and are no longer caught in them. Having seen directly the great way that leads to peace, they are no longer caught in any of the views that exist in the world.

15) When practitioners are not caught in the view "This body is myself," see the ungraspable nature of things and that there is no real existence of a separate self, they have nothing more to be anxious about.

16) When ignorance is uprooted, and all its new shoots have been removed and have no chance to grow again, the practitioner does not cling to anything in their present environment, and there is no longer the need to discriminate between friend and enemy.

17) No longer caught in the concepts of matter and mind as separate from each other, no longer caught in any concept, not seeing anything to grasp, understanding that space and matter are empty, nothing in the three times can make the practitioner complain or be angry.

18) Having completely transcended concepts about everything, including the idea of an object, then you are able to master all the wholesome practices. Having practiced and eloquently taught the teachings of non-desire and nonduality, you are not hesitant in responding to any questions put to you.

19) Having attained understanding, you no longer need to be a follower of anyone. No longer yearning for nor hating anything, you attain inner peace and realize the silence of nirvana.

20) Standing on high, the muni doesn't feel proud. In a lowly position they have no complex. They dwell in equanimity and are not caught in any view. There is no longer any dispute with anyone; hatred and jealousy have ceased. Standing in a place of true insight, they do not feel the slightest pride.

Number 16 of the Arthapada, Taisho 198
(corresponding to Attadaṇḍa Sutta, Sutta Nipāta 935-954)

Discourse on the Enlightened Sage (Muni) (spoken by the Buddha in response to a question from his father)

1. How should those of us who have received the precepts recognize and speak correctly about someone who has right view and has been born as a hero in the world, who has overcome all the fetters and misfortunes? Please Gotama Buddha, teach us.

2. "That person has let go of all hatred and enmity regarding what has happened in the past, and all confusion and worry concerning the future. In the present, they are not attached to anything; to honors or the respect of others.

3. "They do not crave for the future. They do not grieve for the past. On their path of practice, they have let go of all expectations, all wrong views, and they do not hold to any personal opinion.

4. "They have abandoned all fear, have attained stability. They nourish right faith, put an end to all doubts and difficulties. Without envy, they are content with what they have and are fond of the life of freedom.

5. "Able to restrain themselves they are free of ambition. They have much understanding, are jealous of no one, and speak badly of no one. They do not put on an outer appearance. They do not speak divisively and have let go of all useless discussion and doubt.

6. "Their mind is liberated and they do not drown in attachment. They have removed all personal views, do not falsify or embroider the truth, walk peacefully and happily. They have the ability to resolve all disputes, are not carried away by desire, and have put an end to all thoughts of desire.

7. "They do not contrive to attain their own wishes and have no anxiety when they do not possess something. They are not resentful and are not controlled by the sweetness of desire.

8. "They are not proud, they do not see themselves as equal or have an inferiority complex. They know how to look deeply and to practice stopping. They can recognize what is wholesome and what is not, and can let go of wrong perceptions.

9. "Knowing how to look deeply, they see the true nature of all objects of mind and are no longer caught in any of them. They do not need to depend on any object of mind and are not caught in the idea of being or nonbeing.

10. "Mastering desire and stilling their mind, they cross the ocean of grief and arrive at the shore of no worry. They have undone the knots of the internal formations and let go. They have no object of attainment and no longer chase after anything in the three realms.

11. "Not greedy for sons, for farmland, for oxen, not needing possessions, they have nothing more to grasp to or push away.

12. "Even though they are attacked, defamed, harmed, or wrongly condemned by people, even though they are disparaged by brahmans and shramanas, they can sit peacefully, unshakable, and continue on their path of practice.

13. "Without envy and greed, although the world does not respect or revere them, they are not caught. There is no superiority, inferiority, or equality complex. They act according to the Dharma and abandon all that is not according to the Dharma."

14. "Seeing the nature of emptiness, realizing non-expectation and nonattainment, enjoying non-worldly joy, their mind truly stops, and as a muni they transcend concepts of time and space, realize the ultimate dimension and enter the time outside of time."

Arthapada 15, Taisho 198

Discourse on the Emptiness of Formations

This is what I have heard:

Once the Buddha was staying in the Jeta Grove in the Anathapindika monastery in the town of Shravasti. At that time he said to the bhikshus:

"In brief it is like when there is the clapping of two hands, there is a sound; just so when eyes and form condition each other, there is the arising of eyes consciousness. When these three elements (eyes, form, and eyes consciousness) come together, it gives rise to contact. Contact gives rise to feeling. Feeling gives rise to perception and volition.

"All these things are not a self, they are not permanent. If they were a self then that would be an impermanent self, not eternal, not secure, not unchanging. Why is that? Monks, these are things that arise and have to go through birth, decay, and death.

"Monks, all formations are a magic show, like flames. They only last for a bare instant and then they are destroyed; they do not truly come and then go.

"Therefore monks, you should understand thoroughly that such formations are empty. You should accept that they are empty; mindfully observe them. Always remember that they are impermanent, cannot last, and cannot remain for any length of time without changing. They are not the self and they do not belong to a self.

"What is true of the eyes is also true of the ears, nose, tongue, body, and mind. When mind and objects of mind condition each other, mind consciousness arises. When mind, object of mind, and mind consciousness arise, there are contact, feelings, perceptions, and volition. All these things are without a separate self and are impermanent. They are not a self and they do not belong to a self."

Samyukta Āgama 273

Chanda Sutra

Thus have I heard:
At that time there were a number of elder bhikshus staying together in the Deer Park, Rishipatana, near the town of Varanasi, not long after the Buddha had died.

Now the bhikshu Chanda, when it was early morning, put on his sanghati robe, took his bowl, and went into the town of Varanasi to make the alms' round.

When he had made the alms' round and eaten his midday meal, he put away his robe and bowl, and washed his feet. Taking his key with him, he went from one clump of trees to another, from one hut to another, from one walking meditation path to another. Wherever he went he said to the elders:

"Venerable elders, please instruct me, teach me the Dharma so that I can understand the Dharma, see the Dharma, truly know the Dharma, and contemplate the Dharma in the right way."

At that the elder monks said to Chanda:

"Form is impermanent, and feelings, perceptions, mental formations and consciousness are also impermanent. All formations are impermanent, all objects of mind are without a separate self, and nirvana is peace, security, and the silencing (of concepts)."

Chanda said to the elders:

"I know that form is impermanent, and feelings, perceptions, mental formations, and consciousness are also impermanent. I know that all formations are impermanent, all objects of mind are without a separate self and nirvana is peace, security, and the silence of concepts. However, I do not feel happy when I hear that all formations are empty, ungraspable, and that only when sensual desire is ended can nirvana be experienced. If that is so, is there a self (a subject) that is able really to know the truth, and really to see the truth so that the person can say: 'I have seen the Dharma'?"

Chanda repeated his question twice. Then he asked himself: "Who among these elders here can instruct me so that I can understand and see the Dharma?"

Then he thought: "The venerable Ananda is presently staying in the Ghosita Park in the region of Kosambi. He was close to the Buddha and was the Buddha's attendant. The Buddha praised him, and all practitioners of the holy life have heard of him. Surely he will be able to teach me the Dharma so that I can see and understand it."

He rested that night. The next morning, he put on his robe and carrying his bowl went into Varanasi on the alms' round.

After he had completed the alms' round and had the midday meal, he folded his bed. Having folded his bed, he put on his robe, took his bowl, and set out for Kosambi. After many stages of the journey he arrived in Kosambi. Then he put down his bowl and his robe, washed his feet, and went to the place where Ananda was staying. After exchanging courtesies with the venerable monk, Chanda sat down to one side. Then he told Ananda what he had come to ask and said:

"If the time is right, Venerable Ananda, please teach me the Dharma so that I can know and see it."

Then Ananda said to Chanda:

"Good, Chanda! I am glad. I am happy for you that you are able to stand before a practitioner of the holy life and not hide what is in your heart, with the desire of putting an end to the obstacles of doubt in your mind.

"Chanda, ignorant worldly people are not able to understand that form is impermanent, and feelings, perceptions, mental formations, and consciousness are also impermanent. They do not know that all formations are impermanent, all objects of mind are without a separate self, and nirvana is peace, security, and the silence of concepts. Now that you have the capacity to receive the deep and wonderful teachings, listen carefully and I shall instruct you."

Then Chanda thought: "I am happy. I feel a wonderful state of mind, because I know that now I am able to receive the Dharma that is deep and lovely."

Then Ananda said to Chanda:

"I myself heard the Buddha give the following teaching to the Venerable Mahakatyayana:

'People in the world are normally caught in one of two extremes: the view of being and the view of nonbeing. Since worldly people are caught in these two objects of perception, their minds are bound. If someone does not accept, does not grasp, does not stand firm in these perceptions, does not compare and measure a separate self that they are then caught in, then they will see that when the causes are sufficient for suffering to arise, suffering arises, and when the causes are no longer sufficient, suffering ceases (and in that there is no need for a self, and the ideas of being and nonbeing cannot be applied).

"Katyayana, when someone is able to see that, they have no more doubts, they are no longer subject to the afflictions. This insight is not transmitted to them by someone else but is their own insight. This is what the Tathagata means by right view.

"Katyayana, why is this so? When someone looks correctly at the coming to be of the world, they do not give rise to the idea of nonbeing, and when they correctly observe the destruction of the world, they do not give rise to the idea of being. Katyayana, the Tathagata has abandoned these two extremes and teaches the Dharma dwelling in the middle way. This means: This is because that is, and this arises because that arises. Conditioned by ignorance are formations... (and so on until) conditioned by birth are old age, death, sorrow, misfortune, and the afflictions. That is the origin of all this suffering. It also means that this is not because that is not, and this ceases because that ceases. With the ending of ignorance formations cease... (until), with the ending of birth, old age, death, sorrow, misfortune, and the afflictions cease. That is the end of all this suffering."

While Ananda was giving this teaching, Chanda arrived at the state of freedom from the dust of the world. He abandoned all impurities and received the spotless eye of the Dharma. Now he saw and realized the Dharma, knew the Dharma, gave rise to the Dharma, and overcame all doubt. His insight was not given to him by someone else. By listening to this Dharma talk of the Buddha, he attained fearlessness. Respectfully he joined his palms and said to Ananda:

"Indeed, Ananda, you are a true practitioner of the holy life, a spiritual friend, a Dharma teacher who has the capacity to instruct, teach the precepts and the Dharma well.

"Now that I have heard this teaching from the venerable Ananda, I have seen that all objects of mind are empty, are silent and at peace, cannot be grasped conceptually, and only when craving ends and all desire is left behind can there be the absolute peace that is nirvana. My mind is peaceful and happy, dwelling peacefully in liberation. There is no going back, there is no more perception of a separate self. There is only perception of the right Dharma."

Then Ananda said to Chanda:

"Now you have realized something that is of great and wholesome benefit, you have the holy eye of insight into the profound teaching of the Buddha."

Both great beings rejoiced for the other, stood up together, and each returned to his place of abode.

Samyukta Āgama, 262

Invoking the Bodhisattvas' Names

We invoke your name, Avalokiteshvara. We aspire to learn your way of listening in order to help relieve the suffering in the world. You know how to listen in order to understand. We invoke your name in order to practice listening with all our attention and openheartedness. We will sit and listen without any prejudice. We will sit and listen without judging or reacting. We will sit and listen in order to understand. We will sit and listen so attentively that we will be able to hear what the other person is saying and also what is being left unsaid. We know that just by listening deeply we already alleviate a great deal of pain and suffering in the other person.
[BELL]

We invoke your name, Manjushri. We aspire to learn your way, which is to be still and to look deeply into the heart of things and into the hearts of people. We will look with all our attention and openheartedness. We will look with unprejudiced eyes. We will look without judging or reacting. We will look deeply so that we will be able to see and understand the roots of suffering and the impermanent and selfless nature of all that is. We will practice your way of using the sword of understanding to cut through the bonds of suffering, thus freeing ourselves and other species.
[BELL]

We invoke your name, Samantabhadra. We aspire to practice your vow to act with the eyes and heart of compassion, to bring joy to one person in the morning and to ease the pain of one person in the afternoon. We know that the happiness of others is our own happiness, and we aspire to practice joy on the path of service. We know that every word, every look, every action, and every smile can bring happiness to others. We know that if we practice wholeheartedly, we ourselves may become an inexhaustible source of peace and joy for our loved ones and for all species.
[BELL]

We invoke your name, Kshitigarbha. We aspire to learn your way of being present where there is darkness, suffering, oppression, and despair, so we can bring light, hope, relief, and liberation to those places. We are deter-

mined not to forget about or abandon those in desperate situations. We will do our best to establish contact with those who cannot find a way out of their suffering, those whose cries for help, justice, equality, and human rights are not being heard. We know that hell can be found in many places on earth. We will do our best not to contribute to creating more hells on earth, and to help transform the hells that already exist. We will practice in order to realize the qualities of perseverance and stability, so that, like the earth, we can always be supportive, inclusive, and faithful to those in need.
[BELL]

We invoke your name Sadaparibhuta. We aspire to learn your way of looking deeply with the eyes of nondiscrimination in order to see the true qualities of others. Whenever you meet someone, you bow respectfully and say in appreciation *I respect you deeply, for you are a future buddha.* We vow to look deeply into ourselves to recognize the positive qualities that are in us, in order to accept and to love ourselves. We vow to water only the positive seeds in ourselves and in others. Then our thoughts, words, and deeds will give rise to self-confidence and acceptance of ourselves, our children, and all those we know. We vow to look deeply with the eyes of nondiscrimination to see that the joy and success of the other person is also our joy and success. We want to act and to speak with respect and humility. We are determined to practice loving speech to help people who lack confidence in themselves see that they are wonders of the universe. We know that when we are able to remove the barriers of a separate self, we shall be able to transform our complexes of superiority, inferiority, and equality, and realize true happiness and freedom.
[BELL, BELL]

chanto

Chants for Recitation and Meditation

Morning Chant ♪

The Dharma body is shining brightly as the day dawns.
In stillness, we sit.
Our hearts are at peace,
a smile is on our lips.
This is a new day, we vow to go through it in mindfulness,
so the sun of insight can rise
and shine in every direction.
Noble Sangha diligently bring our minds into meditation.

Namo Shakyamunaye Buddhaya
Namo Shakyamunaye Buddhaya
Namo Shakyamunaye Buddhaya

Evening Chant, *Version One* ♪

Stably seated under the Bodhi tree,
body, speech, and mind are one in stillness,
free from views of right and wrong.
When we are focused in perfect mindfulness,
our true nature is illumined.
The shore of confusion is left behind.
Noble Sangha, diligently
we bring our mind into meditation.
Namo Shakyamunaye Buddhaya
Namo Shakyamunaye Buddhaya
Namo Shakyamunaye Buddhaya

Evening Chant, *Version Two* ♪

With posture upright and stable,
we are seated at the foot of the Bodhi tree.
Body, speech, and mind are one in stillness;
there is no more thought of right and wrong.

Our mind and body dwell in perfect mindfulness.
We rediscover our original nature,
leaving the shore of illusion behind.
Noble Sangha, diligently
we bring our mind into meditation.
Namo Shakyamunaye Buddhaya
Namo Shakyamunaye Buddhaya
Namo Shakyamunaye Buddhaya

OPENING VERSE ♪

Namo Tassa Bhagavato Arahato Samma Sambuddhassa
Namo Tassa Bhagavato Arahato Samma Sambuddhassa
Namo Tassa Bhagavato Arahato Samma Sambuddhassa
[BELL]

The Dharma is deep and lovely.
We now have a chance to see, study, and practice it.
We vow to realize its true meaning.
[BELL]

THE SUTRA OF THE INSIGHT
THAT BRINGS US TO THE OTHER SHORE ♪

Avalokiteshvara while practicing deeply
with the insight that brings us to the other shore,
suddenly discovered that all of the five skandhas are equally empty,
and with this realization he overcame all ill-being. [BELL]
"Listen Shariputra, this body itself is emptiness
and emptiness itself is this body.
This body is not other than emptiness
and emptiness is not other than this body.
The same is true of feelings, perceptions,
mental formations, and consciousness. [BELL]

"Listen Shariputra, all phenomena bear the mark of emptiness;
their true nature is the nature of no birth no death,
no being no nonbeing, no defilement no purity,

no increasing no decreasing. [BELL]
"That is why in emptiness, body, feelings,
perceptions, mental formations, and consciousness
are not separate self-entities.
The eighteen realms of phenomena, which are the six sense organs,
six sense objects, and six consciousnesses
are also not separate self-entities.
The Twelve Links of Interdependent Arising
and their extinction are also not separate self-entities.
Ill-being, the causes of ill-being,
the end of ill-being, the path, insight, and attainment,
are also not separate self-entities.
Whoever can see this
no longer needs anything to attain. [BELL]
"Bodhisattvas who practice the insight that brings us to the other shore
see no more obstacles in their mind,
and because there are no more obstacles in their mind,
they can overcome all fear, destroy all wrong perceptions,
and realize perfect nirvana. [BELL]

"All buddhas in the past, present, and future
by practicing the insight that brings us to the other shore
are all capable of attaining authentic and perfect enlightenment. [BELL]

"Therefore Shariputra, it should be known that
the insight that brings us to the other shore is a great mantra
the most illuminating mantra, the highest mantra,
a mantra beyond compare,
the true wisdom that has the power
to put an end to all kinds of suffering. [BELL]
"Therefore let us proclaim a mantra
To praise the insight that brings us to the other shore
Gate Gate Paragate Parasamgate Bodhi Svaha!
Gate Gate Paragate Parasamgate Bodhi Svaha!
Gate Gate Paragate Parasamgate Bodhi Svaha!"
[BELL BELL]

THE THREE REFUGES ♪

I take refuge in the Buddha,
the one who shows me the way in this life.
I take refuge in the Dharma,
the way of understanding and of love.
I take refuge in the Sangha,
the community that lives in harmony and awareness.
[BELL]

Dwelling in the refuge of Buddha,
I clearly see the path of light and beauty in the world.
Dwelling in the refuge of Dharma,
I learn to open many doors on the path of transformation.
Dwelling in the refuge of Sangha,
shining light that supports me, keeping my practice free of obstruction.
[BELL]

Taking refuge in the Buddha in myself,
I aspire to help all people recognize their own awakened nature,
realizing the mind of love.
Taking refuge in the Dharma in myself,
I aspire to help all people fully master the ways of practice
and walk together on the path of liberation.
Taking refuge in the Sangha in myself,
I aspire to help all people build fourfold communities,
to embrace all beings and support their transformation.
[BELL, BELL]

SHARING THE MERIT ♪

Reciting the sutras, practicing the way of awareness
gives rise to benefits without limit.
We vow to share the fruits with all beings.
We vow to offer tribute to parents, teachers, friends, and numerous
 beings
who give guidance and support along the path.
[BELL, BELL, BELL]

PRAISING THE THREE JEWELS ♪

The Buddha jewel shines infinitely.
enlightened for countless lifetimes.
The beauty and stability of Buddha sitting
is seen in the mountains and rivers.
How splendid is the Vulture Peak!
How beautiful the light that shines forth from Buddha's brow,
illumining the six dark paths.
To the Nagapushpa Assembly we will go
to continue the true teachings and practices.
We take refuge in the Buddha ever-present.

The Dharma jewel is infinitely lovely.
the precious words of Buddha,
like fragrant flowers floating down from the heavens.
The wonderful Dharma is plain to see.
It is recorded luminously in three transparent baskets,
from generation to generation handed down in ten directions,
so that today we can see our way.
We vow to learn with all our heart.
We take refuge in the Dharma ever-present.

The Sangha jewel is infinitely precious,
a field of merit and good seeds.
The three robes and begging bowl are symbols of freedom.
The mindfulness trainings, concentration, and insight
support each other.
In mindfulness day and night, the Sangha dwells
and is the foundation for us to realize the fruit of meditation.
With one heart, we come home
and take refuge in the Sangha ever-present.
[BELL, BELL]

Praising the Buddha ♪

The Buddha is like the fresh, full moon
that soars across the immense sky.
When the river of mind is truly calm,
the deep waters perfectly mirror
the radiance of the moon.

The countenance of the World-Honored One,
like the full moon or the orb of the sun,
shines forth bright wisdom's halo
embracing all with love, compassion, joy, and inclusiveness.

May the way of the Buddha grow ever more bright
and all beings receive the Dharma rain.
May compassion cool the flames of the world,
and wisdom shine through the clouds of confusion,
revealing to all the path.
May Mother Earth be protected and safe.
May the people in the world be equal and free.
May the winds and the rains be in harmony.
May the land be at peace in all directions
and the people embrace the path.

May the Sangha practice diligently,
showing love and concern for one and all
just as for our very own family.
Transforming our hearts and minds,
we aspire to follow all great beings.

With one heart we vow to practice the way of all bodhisattvas,
of Samantabhadra and Avalokiteshvara,
the way of perfected wisdom.
[BELL]

Praising Avalokiteshvara

The nectar of compassion is seen on the willow branch
held by the Bodhisattva.
A single drop of this nectar is enough to bring life

to the Ten directions of the cosmos.
May all afflictions of this world disappear totally
and may this place of practice be completely purified
by the Bodhisattva's nectar of compassion.

Homage to the Bodhisattva who refreshes the earth.

From the depths of understanding, a flower of great eloquence blooms.
The Bodhisattva stands majestically
upon the waves of birth and death, free from all afflictions.
Her great compassion eliminates all sickness,
even that once thought of as incurable.
Her wondrous light sweeps away all obstacles and dangers.
Her willow branch, once waved,
reveals countless buddha lands.
Her lotus flower blossoms a multitude of practice centers.
We bow to her. We see her true presence in the here and the now.
We offer her the incense of our hearts.
May the Bodhisattva of Deep Listening embrace us all
with great compassion.

Namo'valokiteshvaraya
[Homage to Bodhisattva Avalokiteshvara]
[BELL]

MAY THE DAY BE WELL ♪

May the day be well and the night be well.
May the midday hour bring happiness too.
In every minute and every second,
may the day and night be well.
By the blessing of the Triple Gem,
may all things be protected and safe.
May all beings born in each of the four ways
live in a land of purity.
May all in the three realms be born upon lotus thrones.
May countless wandering souls
realize the three virtuous positions of the bodhisattva path.
May all living beings, with grace and ease,
fulfill the bodhisattva stages.

The countenance of the World-Honored One, like the full moon
or like the orb of the sun, shines with the light of clarity.
A halo of wisdom spreads in every direction,
enveloping all with love and compassion,
joy and equanimity.

Namo Shakyamunaye Buddhaya
Namo Shakyamunaye Buddhaya
Namo Shakyamunaye Buddhaya
[BELL, BELL]

WE ARE TRULY PRESENT ♪

With hearts established in mindfulness, we are truly present
for sitting and walking meditation, and for reciting the sutras.
May this practice center, with its fourfold sangha,
be supported by the Three Jewels and Holy Beings,
well-protected from the eight misfortunes
and the three paths of suffering.

May parents, teachers, friends, and all beings within the three realms
be filled with the most divine grace,
and may it be found that in the world there is no place at war.
May the winds be favorable, the rains seasonable,
and the peoples' hearts at peace.
May the practice of the noble community, diligent and steady,
ascend the Ten Bodhisattva Stages with ease and energy.
May the Sangha body live peacefully, fresh and full of joy,
a refuge for all, offering happiness and insight.

The wisdom of the Awakened Mind shines out like the full moon.
The body of the Awakened One is pure and clear as crystal.
In the world the Awakened One relieves bitterness and suffering.
In every place the Awakened Mind reveals love and compassion.

Namo Shakyamunaye Buddhaya
Namo Shakyamunaye Buddhaya
Namo Shakyamunaye Buddhaya
[BELL, BELL]

THE FOUR RECOLLECTIONS ♪

The Blessed One is worthy and fully self-awakened.
I bow before the Buddha.
[BELL]

The teaching is well expounded by the Blessed One.
I pay homage to the Dharma.
[BELL]

The community of the Blessed One's disciples has practiced well.
I pay respect to the Sangha.
[BELL]

The Noble Teacher in whom I take refuge
is the one who embodies and reveals the ultimate reality,
is the one who is worthy of all respect and offerings,
is the one who is endowed with perfected wisdom,
is the one who is endowed with right understanding and
compassionate action,
is the one who happily crossed to the shore of freedom,
is the one who looked deeply to know the world well,
is the highest charioteer training humankind,
teaching gods and humans,
the Awakened One, the World-Honored One.
[BELL]

The teaching given by my Noble Teacher
is the path I undertake, the teaching well-proclaimed,
is the teaching that can be realized right here and right now,
is the teaching that is immediately useful and effective,
is the teaching inviting all to come and see directly,
is the teaching that is leading to the good, the true, the beautiful,
extinguishing the fire of afflictions;
it is a teaching for all sensible people to realize for themselves.
[BELL]

Practicing the teachings, the noble community in which I take refuge
is the community that goes in the direction of goodness,

in the direction of truth,
in the direction of beauty,
in the direction of righteousness;
is the community that is composed of four pairs and eight kinds
of holy people;
is the community that is worthy of offerings, worthy of great respect,
worthy of admiration, worthy of salutation;
is the community standing upon the highest fields of merit in all
of the world.
[BELL]

The mindfulness trainings, the wholesome way of living taught by
Noble Teacher,
is the wonderful practice that remains unbroken,
that remains harmonious, that remains flawless, that remains refined;
is the wonderful practice that has the capacity to prevent wrongdoing
and to prevent danger;
is the wonderful practice that has the capacity to protect self and others
and to reveal beauty;
is the wonderful practice that is leading to concentration, leading to
peacefulness, leading to insight, leading to non-fear;
is the wonderful practice that shows us the way to total emancipation
and long-lasting happiness.
[BELL] [BELL]

THE REFUGE CHANT ♪

Incense perfumes the atmosphere.
A lotus blooms and the Buddha appears.
The world of suffering and discrimination
is filled with the light of the rising sun.
As the dust of fear and anxiety settles,
with open heart, one-pointed mind,
I turn to the Three Jewels.
[BELL]

The Fully Enlightened One, beautifully seated, peaceful and smiling,
a living source of understanding and compassion,
to the Buddha I go for refuge.
[BELL]

The path of mindful living,
leading to healing, joy, and enlightenment, the way of peace,
to the Dharma I go for refuge.
[BELL]

The loving and supportive community of practice,
realizing harmony, awareness, and liberation,
to the Sangha I go for refuge.
[BELL]

I am aware that the Three Gems are within my heart.
I vow to realize them,
practicing mindful breathing and smiling,
looking deeply into things.
I vow to understand living beings and their suffering,
to cultivate compassion and loving kindness,
to practice joy and equanimity.
[BELL]

I vow to offer joy to one person in the morning,
to help relieve the grief of one person in the afternoon,
living simply and sanely with few possessions,
keeping my body healthy.
I vow to let go of all worries and anxiety
in order to be light and free.
[BELL]

I am aware that I owe so much
to my parents, teachers, friends, and all beings.
I vow to be worthy of their trust, to practice wholeheartedly
so that understanding and compassion will flower,
helping living beings be free from their suffering.
May the Buddha, the Dharma, and the Sangha
support my efforts.
[BELL, BELL]

NOURISHING HAPPINESS

Sitting here in this moment, protected by the Sangha,
we see how fortunate we are.
We have been born human,
and encountered the Dharma.
The seed of bodhicitta has been watered,
and we have the conditions to live in harmony in the Sangha.

The energy of the Sangha, the mindfulness trainings, and fine manners
are protecting and helping us not make mistakes,
so that unwholesome action does not take us on dark paths.
With kind spiritual friends, we are on the path of goodness,
illumined by the light of buddhas and bodhisattvas.
(Bell)

Although seeds of suffering are still in us
in the form of afflictions and habit energies,
mindfulness can always manifest, helping us touch
what is wonderful within and around us.

We are grateful for our six senses:
our eyes that can see the blue sky,
our ears that can hear the birds singing,
our nose that smells the scent of sandalwood,
our tongue that tastes the nectar of the Dharma.
Our posture is stable,
and our mind is one with our body.

If there were not a World-Honored One,
if there were not the wonderful Dharma,
if there were not the Sangha,
we would not be so fortunate
to enjoy this Dharma happiness today.

We vow to cultivate and maintain our practice,
for our ancestors, family, future generations, and society.
Our resources for practice are our own peace and joy.
We vow to cultivate and nourish them by our daily mindfulness.

In our society countless people are suffering,
drowning in sensual pleasure, jealousy, and hatred.
Aware of this situation, we are determined to practice
to master the mental formations of craving and anger,
to train to be able to listen deeply and use loving speech
in order to restore communication and create understanding, acceptance,
and love.

Just like the bodhisattvas,
we vow to practice looking at everyone around us
with the eyes of compassion and a heart of understanding.
We vow to listen with a clear mind and ears of compassion,
bringing peace and joy into the lives of others,
to lighten and alleviate the suffering of living beings.

I am aware that ignorance and wrong perceptions
can turn this world into a fiery hell.
I vow to walk always upon the path of transformation,
producing understanding and loving kindness,
and cultivating a garden of awakening.

Although there are birth, sickness, old age, and death,
now that I have a path of practice, I have nothing more to fear.
It is a great happiness to be alive in the Sangha
and with the practice of mindfulness trainings and concentration,
to live every moment in stability and freedom;
to take part in the work of relieving others' suffering,
the career of buddhas and bodhisattvas.

In each precious moment, I am filled with deep gratitude.
I bow before the World-Honored One.
Please bear witness to my wholehearted gratitude,
and embrace all beings with arms of great compassion.
[BELL, BELL]

TURNING TO THE TATHAGATA

I touch the earth and turn to the Tathagata,
the lighthouse that shines over the ocean of dust and suffering.
Lord of Compassion, embrace us with your love.
Today we are determined to return to our true home.

We, your disciples, owe so much gratitude
to our parents, teachers, friends, and all other beings,
which we have not been able to repay.
Looking over the three realms and across the four quarters,
we see all species drowning in suffering.
It wakes us with a start.
Although we have turned in its direction,
the shore of awakening still lies far away.
Fortunately, everywhere in the saha world
are the hands of the Compassionate One bringing relief.
[BELL]

We wholeheartedly return and take refuge,
vowing to be disciples of the Tathagata.
We unify our body and mind before the Buddha,
letting go of all our worldly desires.
With great respect, we shall receive the wonderful teachings,
and put them into practice every day,
nourishing mindfulness trainings and concentration,
for the fruit of understanding to be ripened in the future.
May the practice protect us day and night.
May the Buddha, Dharma, and Sangha show us their compassion.

We know that the obstacles created by our actions are still heavy,
that the merit from our virtues is still frail,
that our perceptions are still often wrong,
that our roots of understanding are not yet solid,
that the impurities of our mind still arise easily,
that our listening, contemplation, and practice are not really firm.
In this moment, we touch the earth,
may loving kindness embrace us as we open our hearts.
[BELL]

We, your disciples for countless past lives,
have chased after worldly things,
because we have not been able to recognize our pure, original mind.
Our actions of body, speech, and mind have been unwholesome.
We have drowned in ignorant cravings, jealousy, hatred, and anger.
Now the sound of the great bell has awoken us,
and we are determined to renew our body and mind,
to completely remove all wrongdoings.

In this moment,
we make the deep vow to leave behind old habit energies,
taking refuge in the Sangha for our whole life.
May loving kindness and compassion support us.

We vow that while we meditate, share the Dharma,
stand, walk, cook, wash the dishes,
lie, sit, work, wash clothes,
and practice slow walking,
while we recollect the buddhas and bodhisattvas,
offer incense or touch the earth,
every step will restore peace and joy,
every smile will radiate freedom.
We will live mindfully in each and every moment
in order to show people there is a path out of suffering.

We vow to touch the Pure Land with every step
and the ultimate dimension in every action.
We shall take steps on the ground of reality,
breathe to realize true emptiness,
lighting up the clear wisdom of the wonderful mind
and drawing aside the curtain of ignorance.
May our body and mind be pure and happy, free and at ease,
so that when we leave this life,
we shall be free from regrets and pain,
our mind will be conscious,
with clear mindfulness and the six senses calmed,
we shall let go of this body in meditative concentration.
[BELL]

In our next manifestation
we shall be disciples of the Tathagata,
continuing the career of helping the world,
bringing all species to the shore of awakening,
realizing the Three Bodies and the Four Wisdoms,
using the Five Eyes and the Six Miracles,
manifesting thousands of appropriate forms,
being present at the same time in the Three Worlds,
coming in and going out in freedom.
We will not abandon anyone, helping all beings to transform,
and bringing them to the shore of no regression.

Space, living beings, actions, and afflictions are infinite.
My aspiration is also infinite.
We bow before the Buddha and vow to practice
to uphold virtue and share this merit with countless beings,
in order to repay the gratitude that we owe
and bring the teachings of transformation everywhere.

May we, along with all beings,
fully realize the great understanding.
[BELL, BELL]

PROTECTING AND TRANSFORMING

We, your disciples, who from beginningless time
have created so many obstacles out of ignorance,
being born and dying with no direction,
have now found confidence in the highest awakening.
However much we may have drifted on the ocean of suffering,
today we see clearly that there is a beautiful path.
We turn toward the light of loving kindness to direct us.
We bow deeply to the Awakened One and to our spiritual ancestors
who light up the path before us, guiding every step.
[BELL]

The wrongdoings and sufferings in our life
are brought about by craving, hatred, ignorance, and pride.
Today we begin anew to purify and free our hearts.

With awakened wisdom, bright as the sun and the full moon,
and immeasurable compassion to help beings,
we resolve to live a wholesome life.
With all our heart, we go for refuge to the Three Jewels.
With the boat of loving kindness,
we cross over the ocean of suffering.
With the torch of insight, we leave behind the forest of confusion.
With determination, we learn, reflect, and practice.
Right View is the ground of our actions of body, speech, and mind.
We walk, stand, lie down, and sit in mindfulness.
Upright and dignified, we speak, smile, come in, and go out.

Whenever anger or anxiety enters our heart,
we are determined to breathe mindfully and come back to ourselves.
With every step, we walk in the Pure Land.
With every look, we see the Dharmakaya.
Diligent and attentive,
we guard our six senses as they touch sense objects.
We transform old habit energies
so that the heart's garden of awakening
blooms with hundreds of flowers.
We bring peace and joy to every household,
and plant wholesome seeds on countless paths.
We aspire to remain with the Sangha,
in order to help beings everywhere in the world.

May mountains and rivers be our witness in this moment
as we bow our heads
and request the Lord of Compassion to embrace us.
[BELL, BELL]

LOVING SPEECH AND DEEP LISTENING

Coming back to myself,
I kneel at the foot of the lotus throne
and admire the spiritual light
that shines from the face of the World Honored One.
The Tathagata is immeasurable space and the light of dawn,
the solid planet that carries us
as we return from the world of confusion
to unobstructed inclusiveness.
(BELL)

For so many past lifetimes, we have made mistakes,
which have brought about much suffering.
There are times we cannot look at each other
Because we hold on to internal formations.
We lose our capacity to listen deeply
and to speak loving, harmonious words.
The communication between us is blocked.
We have no way to resolve our suffering.
Every day, understanding and love are less present.
The heavy, stifling atmosphere smothers all our joy.
To express my resolve I touch the earth,
and vow to follow the teachings of the Tathagata.
I shall begin to practice listening deeply and speaking lovingly,
according to the Dharma doors of helpfulness and empathy
so that communication can be quickly restored.
(BELL)

I shall practice diligently to guard my body and mind
by conscious breathing and awareness of my steps,
so that I can recognize and embrace
the anger and irritation in my heart;
so I can sit and listen deeply with all my compassion,
so the other person has a chance to share
the suffering they have repressed.
I want to learn to listen deeply
with sincere loving kindness
so that the other person can suffer less.

I promise the Buddha
that even if the other person says things that are not true,
even if their words contain blame,
I shall continue to listen attentively.
I shall wait for the right time
to find a way to let the other person know
what really happened,
so they have a chance to rectify their perceptions.
I want to practice harmonious and loving speech
to help the person sitting with me
hear and understand what I want to say.
Whenever I feel some irritation,
I shall just practice breathing and walking meditation,
and above all, avoid any argument.
I vow only to speak
when I am able to master my mind.

I ask the World-Honored One,
the Bodhisattva of Great Understanding Manjushri,
the Bodhisattva of Great Action, Samantabhadra,
and the Bodhisattva of Great Compassion, Avalokita,
to support and shine light for me,
so that I can soon be successful on the path of practice.
[BELL, BELL]

REPENTANCE AND TAKING REFUGE FOR LIFE

With our whole life, we go for refuge
to the awakened ones in the ten directions,
to the deep and wonderful Dharma which has been proclaimed,
and to the holy Sangha which realizes the four fruits
and practices the three vehicles of liberation.
In compassion, please stretch out your arms to protect us.
[BELL]

For a long time, we have gone against the stream of our true nature,
floundering in the ocean of sorrows and the river of confusion,
unable to see a way out or a path to our true home.
Bobbing up and down on the waves,
we have not been able to turn around.
We have laid down the conditions for the formation of afflictions.
Over so many lifetimes, we have committed actions that hindered us.
We have not been able to distinguish the straight path from the crooked.
The retribution of our resentment is heavy.
Now we sincerely bow our heads.
Relying on great compassion, we open our hearts to begin anew.
[BELL]

Sincerely we call on the great capacity to love
to rescue us with all beings from the ocean of birth and death.
With good spiritual friends,
we are determined to leave behind our afflictions
and reach the shore of liberation.
In this life we vow to strengthen our merit and practice.
May our career of practice be fully realized so that
understanding and love spring up fresh and lovely.
In the next life, may we be born human beings,
and may we meet the teachings and live a life of true practice.

May we be guided on the path by an enlightened teacher.
Relying on true faith, may we practice the monastic path.
May our six senses be clear and three actions in harmony.
May we not run after and be caught in the ways of the world.

Wholeheartedly and diligently,
we preserve the holy life and are free from worldly concerns.
May our fine manners and conduct shine brightly.
With loving kindness, may we protect the life of even the smallest beings.
May we bring about wholesome conditions
so that countless misfortunes can dissipate like the morning mist.
With all our heart, we give rise to the bodhicitta
so the true understanding of emptiness may manifest.
With our diligent practice,
may we awaken to the highest truth
and be capable of transmitting the true mind.
May we go beyond the cycle of rebirth,
developing tthe Six Paramitas in order to rescue beings.
May we build practice centers everywhere
so that the net of doubt is destroyed near and far.
May we subdue all unwholesome temptations,
transmitting the Dharma lamp and continuing the lineage infinitely.
May we engage in the career of the buddhas in the ten directions,
not discouraged because of weariness or toil.
However many deep and wonderful Dharma doors there are,
may we realize them all to awaken ourselves,
and then bring that merit and wisdom to awaken others,
realizing the fruit of buddhahood and the Dharmakaya.

[BELL]

May we respond to circumstances in the world,
realizing numberless bodies to help beings.
May the nectar of loving kindness rain on the realm of gods and men
so that the ocean of actions and vows to rescue beings becomes vast.
May all places near and far be in harmony.
By proclaiming the wonderful Dharma may we rescue all beings.
We will manifest and bring light to the dark realms.
May those who are imprisoned in suffering
be free when seeing us or hearing our name.
May we give rise to our deepest aspiration
so that the suffering of ten thousand realms will dissipate.
By our deep determination,

may the wrong actions leading to unspeakable injustice
and suffering for all animals
vanish like the morning dew on the green mountain.

May we give medicines to the sick
and food and clothes to the destitute.
May we realize the benefits of these actions,
and peace and joy right in the cycle of samsara.
Together with all those we have known, whether dear to us or not,
may we vow to cross over the ocean of afflictions.
May we leave behind unwholesome attachments forever,
and untie the internal formations of body and mind.
May we cultivate the path of wholesome action
and together with all species go towards the Dharmakaya.

Even if the heavens were to move,
our vows will not be shaken for countless lifetimes.
May all beings from time immemorial
fulfill the career of great understanding
and strengthen the tree of awakening.
[BELL, BELL]

HAPPINESS IN THE PRESENT MOMENT

The Buddha has taught:
"The past has already gone,
and the future has not yet come.
Do not let your mind drown in regret for the past
or anxiety for the future."
The Buddha teaches:
"You can live peacefully and in freedom in this present moment."
Let us hear the Buddha's words
and let go of our sadness and anxiety.
Let us come back to ourselves
and establish ourselves in what is present right now.
Let us learn to recognize the conditions for happiness
that are present within us and around us.

Can we hear the birds singing

and the wind in the pines?
Can we see the green mountains,
the white clouds, the golden moon?
The Pure Land is available in the present moment.
Every day we can enjoy ourselves in the Buddha Land.
Every mindful breath and step take us to the Pure Land,
revealing all the wonders of the Dharma body.

I am determined to abandon
the habits of being in a hurry and competing.
I shall not run after fame, power, riches, and sex,
because I know that this does not lead to true happiness.
All it will bring me is misery and misfortune.

I shall learn to know what is sufficient,
to live simply,
so that I have time to live deeply
every moment of my daily life,
giving my body and mind a chance to heal,
and to have the time to look after and protect
those I have vowed to love.

I shall practice for my mind to grow in love and compassion,
so that I have the ability to help beings anywhere
who are drowning in craving.

I ask the Buddhas everywhere
to protect and guide me,
to support me on my path,
so that I can live in peace, joy, and freedom every day,
fulfilling my deepest aspiration as your disciple
whom you trust and love.
[BELL, BELL]

WATERING SEEDS OF JOY ♪

My mother, my father, are in me.
And when I look, I see myself in them.

The Buddha, the patriarchs, are in me.
And when I look, I see myself in them.
I am a continuation
of my mother, my father, and my ancestors.
It is my aspiration
to preserve and continue to nourish
seeds of goodness, skill, and happiness
which I have inherited.
It is also my desire to recognize
the seeds of fear and suffering I have inherited,
and, bit by bit, to transform them.

I am a continuation
of the Buddha and my spiritual teachers.
It is my deep aspiration
to preserve, nourish, and develop
the seeds of understanding, love, and freedom
which they have transmitted to me.

I desire to continue
the career of the Buddha and my ancestral teachers,
and do my best to realize
all that the Buddha and my ancestral teachers expect of me.

In my daily life, I also want to sow
seeds of love and compassion
in my own consciousness
and in the heart of other people.
I am determined not to water
seeds of craving, aversion, and violence
in myself and in others.

I know that if I practice
all this in the right way,

after only seven days,
I shall already have been able
to change the situation,
re-establish communication,
smile and transform suffering
and increase my happiness.

Please, Lord Buddha,
be witness to what is in my heart.
With mind and body in perfect unity,
I bow my head and touch the earth.
[BELL, BELL]

AWAKENING THE SOURCE OF LOVE

We bow respectfully to Avalokiteshvara,
to your great vow always to be there for all beings,
your capacity to look deeply at the world with compassionate eyes,
listen deeply to understand and to relieve suffering,
and with your willow branch,
to sprinkle the sacred nectar of immortality,
cleansing my mind from all impurities.
I vow to take refuge in you with all my heart.
Respectfully, I offer you my deepest vow:
[BELL]

Namo 'valokiteshvaraya,
I vow to look deeply into the five skandhas.
Namo 'valokiteshvaraya,
I vow to see the true nature of emptiness.
Namo 'valokiteshvaraya,
I vow soon to reach the shore of awakening.
Namo 'valokiteshvaraya,
I vow to overcome all obstacles.
Namo 'valokiteshvaraya,
I vow to take the boat of Perfect understanding.

Namo 'valokiteshvaraya,
I vow to be present in all three bodies.

Namo 'valokiteshvaraya,
I vow to realize the fruits of liberation.
Namo 'valokiteshvaraya,
I vow to cultivate great compassion.
Namo 'valokiteshvaraya,
I vow to penetrate deeply the Tathagata store.
Namo 'valokiteshvaraya,
I vow to purify my mind.
[BELL]

Namo 'valokiteshvaraya,
may I be free from the abyss of craving.
Namo 'valokiteshvaraya,
may I break through the shell of my worldly mind.
Namo 'valokiteshvaraya,
may I have sufficient skillful means.
Namo 'valokiteshvaraya,
may I build Sangha.
Namo 'valokiteshvaraya,
may I transform my anger.
Namo 'valokiteshvaraya,
may I uproot my ignorance.
Namo 'valokiteshvaraya,
may I hold high the torch of right faith.
Namo 'valokiteshvaraya,
may I have the clear eyes of understanding.
Namo 'valokiteshvaraya,
may I hold the golden lotus in my hand.
Namo 'valokiteshvaraya,
may I see the Dharma body.
[BELL]

Namo 'valokiteshvaraya,
I vow to build brotherhood and sisterhood.
Namo 'valokiteshvaraya,
I vow to show gratitude to my spiritual lineage.
Namo 'valokiteshvaraya,
I vow to practice loving speech.

Namo 'valokiteshvaraya,
I vow to look with loving eyes.
Namo 'valokiteshvaraya,
I vow to succeed in my practice of deep listening.
Namo 'valokiteshvaraya,
I vow to live mindfully and with clarity.
Namo 'valokiteshvaraya,
I vow soon to realize meditative concentration.
Namo 'valokiteshvaraya,
I vow to walk solidly night and day.
Namo 'valokiteshvaraya,
I vow to abide peacefully on the ground of reality.
Namo 'valokiteshvaraya,
I vow to cultivate the five eyes, and the six miraculous powers.
[BELL]

Namo 'valokiteshvaraya,
please come with me to the war zones
to stop the killing and bombing.
Please walk with me to the places of sickness and suffering,
bringing medicine and the refreshing nectar of compassion.
Please come with me to the realm of the hungry ghosts,
bringing the Dharma food of understanding and love.
Please come with me to the realm of hell
in order to cool the heat of afflictions.
Please come with me to places of conflict
in order to remove hatred and anger
and help the source of love to flow again.

Homage to the Bodhisattva of Great Compassion
Homage to the Bodhisattva of Great Compassion
Homage to the Bodhisattva of Great Compassion
[BELL, BELL]

MASTERING ANGER

I bow my head and touch the earth
before the highest charioteer who trains humankind.

Stretch out your arms of compassion;
bring us to the shore of peace and solidity.
For so long, confusion has inhabited us
so that we have not had the chance to learn,
and we have often acted foolishly,
allowed seeds of anger and violence
to be watered in our deep consciousness.

Whenever seeds of irritation or annoyance
arise and operate in my mind,
they always cause wounds and resentment
in myself and in so many others.

Listening to Avalokita's teaching,
I begin right now with a deep aspiration:
whenever anger arises,
I shall come back to myself,
taking refuge in my mindful breathing and steps
so as to look after and embrace,
to protect and recognize
the painful mental formations in me.

I shall remember to look deeply
to see the true nature and source of hatred and anger.
Heeding the Buddha's teachings,
I shall know how to guard my mind.
When anger arises in me
I shall not do or say anything
until I have mastered it.
I shall look deeply to see
the real nature of my pain.
[BELL]

The seed of ignorance
is the cause of my suffering,
and the reason why the seed of anger in me has grown so strong.
Those who make me angry
have so much suffering themselves.

They have not been able
to come home to themselves to guard their mind.
They do not know how to transform
the deep-seated habit energies within.

Contemplating in this way,
I will be able to bring about understanding and acceptance,
and help the other person
to practice and to transform the suffering within them.

The World-Honored One has taught:
When we are able to master our anger,
we bring a double victory to ourself and to the other person.

I want to practice with all my heart
in order to repay my gratitude to the great favor.
May the Three Jewels embrace us with loving kindness
so that we can quickly cross over to the shore of peace and happiness.
[BELL, BELL]

JOYFULLY SHARING THE MERIT ♪

Blessèd Ones who dwell in the world, grant to us compassion.
In this and countless lives before, from beginningless time,
our mistakes have caused much suffering to ourselves and others.
We have done wrong, encouraged others to do wrong,
and given our consent to acts of killing, stealing, deceiving,
sexual misconduct, and other harmful actions
among the Ten Unwholesome Deeds.
Whether our faults are known to others or whether they are hidden,
they have brought us to the realms of hell, hungry ghosts, and animals,
causing us to be born in places filled with pain and suffering.
We have not yet had the chance to realize our full potential.
Today we are determined, with one-pointed concentration,
to repent the obstacles of our past unwholesome actions.
[BELL]

Blessèd Ones, be our witness and look upon us with compassion.
We surrender before you and make this aspiration:

If at all within this very life and countless lives before,
we have given, even if only a handful of food or simple garment;
if we have ever spoken kindly, even if only a few words;
if we have ever looked with eyes of compassion,
even if only for a moment;
if we have ever comforted or consoled, even if only once or twice;
if we have ever listened carefully to wonderful teachings,
even if only to one talk;
if we have ever offered a meal to monks and nuns, even if only once;
if we have ever saved a life, even if only that of an ant or a worm;
if we have ever recited a sutra, even if only one or two lines;
if we have ever been a monk or a nun, even if only for one life;
if we have ever supported others on the path of practice,
even if only two or three people;
if we have ever observed the mindfulness trainings,
even if imperfectly;
all of this merit has slowly formed wholesome seeds within us.
Today we gather them together like a fragrant flower garland
and, with great respect, we offer it to all awakened ones —
a contribution to the fruit of the highest path.
[BELL]

Opening our hearts wide to the Perfect Highest Awakening,
we are resolved to attain great understanding.
We will realize compassion and embody deep love.
We will practice diligently, transforming our suffering
and the suffering of all other species.
Please transfer the merits of body, speech, and mind
to the happiness of people and all other beings.
Apart from bodhicitta and apart from the thirst
for great understanding and the embodiment of love,
there is no other desire within us.
All buddhas in the three times and the ten directions
have offered their merit as we are doing today.
Repenting all our faults, we joyfully contribute
to the immeasurable ocean of merit
and the towering peaks of the highest understanding.
The buddhas and the ancestral teachers
are the light which shows us the way.

In this solemn moment, with all our life's force,
we come back to ourselves and bow deeply with respect.
[BELL, BELL]

BEGINNING ANEW CHANT

I, your disciple
with my heart at peace and pure,
join my palms as a lotus bud
and turn respectfully to you
the Great hero of loving kindness,
and conqueror of afflictions, Shakyamuni Buddha,
as I offer words of fervent repentance.
[BELL]

I was not fortunate enough
to bring the teachings into my life earlier
and so lived in forgetfulness for a long time.
Obscured by ignorance, I have brought about suffering
and have made many foolish mistakes.
I and my ancestors
have sown our heart's garden with unwholesome seeds.
We have been responsible for killing, stealing,
sexual misconduct, and wrong speech.
Much of what we have said and done
has continued to do damage day after day.
I repent of these countless afflictions
that have obstructed my happiness.
I vow to begin anew from today.
[BELL]

I see I have been thoughtless
and wandered from the path of mindfulness.
Ignorance and afflictions have accumulated in me
and created feelings of hatred and grief.
My mind is sometimes weary of life
and troubled by anxiety.
Because I have not understood others
I have been angry and resentful,

arguing and blaming,
courting suffering every day,
making greater the rift between us.
There are days when we do not want
to speak to or look at each other,
and the internal knots last a long time.
Now I turn to the Three Jewels.
In sincere repentance I bow my head.
[BELL]

I know that in my consciousness
are buried countless wholesome seeds of love and understanding
and of peace and joy.
But because I have not known how to water them
the wholesome seeds have not sprouted fresh and green.
Overwhelmed by suffering
I have made my life dark.
I have grown used to chasing a distant happiness.
My mind is constantly occupied by the past
or travelling far into the future.
I am caught in a cycle of anger.
Unable to appreciate the precious things I have,
I trample on real happiness,
so suffering is there month after month, year after year.
Now before the altar fragrant with incense,
I vow to change and begin anew.
[BELL]

With sincerity and respect,
I turn to the buddhas in the ten directions
and the bodhisattvas, the hearer disciples,
self-awakened buddhas, and the holy ones.
With deep regret I repent my repeated mistakes.
May the nectar of purity
extinguish the flames of my afflictions.
May the boat of the true Dharma
carry me out of resentment.
I vow to live in an awakened way,
to train according to the true teachings that have been transmitted.

I vow to practice mindful breathing and smiling
and diligently live in mindfulness.
[BELL]

I vow to come back to myself
and live in the wonderful present moment,
to sow wholesome seeds in my heart's garden,
cultivating understanding and love.
I vow to learn to look deeply
and practice deep understanding,
to see the true nature of all that is
and free myself from the suffering
brought about by the notion of birth and death.
I vow to practice loving speech,
to love and care for others throughout the day,
bringing the source of joy to many places,
helping people to suffer less,
and repaying the deep gratitude I owe
to parents, teachers, and friends.
With faith I light up the incense of my heart.
I turn to the Compassionate One
and ask for protection on the wonderful path of practice.
I vow to train myself diligently
so that the fruits of the path can ripen.
[BELL, BELL]

IN PRAISE OF MOTHER EARTH

Homage to the Refreshing Earth Bodhisattva
Mother of this world and all beings.
We turn to you with deep admiration,
Beautiful blue planet in the immensity of space.
You have given birth to countless species,
Manifesting so many wonders of life,
Loving unconditionally without discrimination,
Embracing all species without exception.

Tender, generous, and stable,
You are the mother holding all beings.

Countless bodhisattvas spring up
From your fresh green cradle.
You embrace, transform, and dispel all hatred,
Creating and nourishing day and night,
For your lap to bloom with flowers of the Sun.

Your heart opens to thousands of galaxies,
As you share your joy with the trichiliocosm,
Seeing the interbeing nature of all that is,
Conserving and protecting so that nothing is lost.
There is no being or non-being, no eternity or annihilation,
No sameness or difference, no coming or going.
Your love is boundless,
Your virtues are impeccable.
Your love is the love of the Four Immeasurable Minds,
As vast and full as the four great oceans.

With each spring you don a new robe:
The red roses, the green willow, so beautiful and fresh.
When summer comes
thousands of plants display a symphony of deep colors,
Offering a bounty of rich seeds and sweet fruits.
The autumn forest radiates with color,
And when winter arrives beautiful snowflakes grace the sky.
At dusk, the sound of the rising tide rolls like thunder;
At dawn, the beauty of the sunrise is beyond compare,
Revealing the splendours of the universe.
You are the most beautiful jewel of the solar system,
The wisdom that lights up the ten directions,
A heart that is open to all places.
Mother Earth, you are the Pure Land of the present moment,
And you are the future of all species.
We come back and take refuge in you,
No longer searching, no longer running.
We realize that you are always there within us and
And that we continue in you for eternity.
May we be inspired by your example,
And live deeply every moment with peace and joy.

Homage to the Refreshing Earth Bodhisattva
Homage to the Refreshing Earth Bodhisattva
Homage to the Refreshing Earth Bodhisattva.

PRAISING THE BUDDHA OF LIGHT

We bow before the Buddha of Infinite Light,
Whose energy radiates across ten thousand worlds.
We have a chance today
To hear your wonderful call.

We bow before the Buddha of Immortality,
Manifesting as the shining orb of the great sun.
We are children of the sun
And you light our way.

The great earth is our home.
This beautiful blue planet
Is nothing less than a beloved mother,
Whose orbit is an orbit of love
In a celestial walking meditation through the solar system.

The radiating light of the Great Tathagata Sun
Is the source of life on earth.
Wherever there is life,
There is the Great Tathagata Sun.
The radiating light of the Great Tathagata Sun
Nourishes all life on earth.
Wherever we go, we can find our way
Thanks to your limitless light.

The limitless energy of Great Tathagata Sun
Makes possible the white clouds and golden moon,
The high mountains and vast rivers,
Flowing into the clear blue waters of the four great oceans.

The energy of the Buddha of Immortality,
Brings to life the green willow and the red plum blossom,

The golden chrysanthemums and the violet bamboo,
And reveals the wonderful dharmakaya.

The Great Tathagata Sun embraces the earth,
Creating this peaceful Pure Land,
So that numerous great beings can assemble
and build communities of peace.

Just as buddha nature does not discriminate
Between north and south,
The Pure Land is not bound
By east or west.
The Awakened One has compassionately taught
That the Pure Land is in the very here and now.

We vow to walk on the ground of reality,
To be aware of our body,
To touch the earth with every step,
To see the wonders of life at every moment,
To see the nature of no birth and no death,
To see the nature of no coming and no going,
To remove the net of illusion
And light up the torch of wisdom,
To see that the saha world is also the Pure Land,
To recognize that afflictions are the awakening,
To touch nirvana in the heart of samsara,
To reach the shore of awakening
And transform the roots of ignorance.

Every step we take on Mother Earth
helps us be in touch with Father Sun.
With every step taken in peace and joy,
Thousands of flowers bloom across the earth.

The Dharma nectar has manifested,
The Dharma nectar has appeared,
The Dharma nectar returns amidst this glorious sky,
The Dharma nectar advances in splendor.

The Pure Land of the present is so wonderful,
Seen in the white clouds and blue sky.
Buddhas in ten thousand directions bear witness
And join their voices
To praise the Buddha of Limitless Light.

May our actions of body, speech and mind,
Contribute to a healthy and peaceful world,
And train bodhisattvas who will become future Buddhas
And help prevent the tragedy of war.

We vow to live in mindfulness,
To wholeheartedly protect our beautiful planet.
We vow to build a strong and healthy sangha,
and to continue the Buddha's work to rescue all beings.

We vow to look deeply
To see the interdependent nature of all that is,
To realize the insight of signlessness,
And see beyond the outer forms,
To be in touch with the true nature of reality,
and see that there is no birth and no death,
so we can overcome all fear
and touch true peace.

May the Buddha of Infinite Light and Life embrace us,
May Buddha Shakyamuni be our witness,
And support us, your disciples, to successfully realize our path.

Namo Buddha Amitabha
Namo Buddha Vairocana
Namo Buddha Shakyamuni

GIVING RISE TO OUR ASPIRATION

Taking refuge in Amitabha,
in the wonderful ultimate dimension.
I am determined to return to myself

and maintain the source of mindfulness.
My aspiration is to come back
and take refuge in Amitabha.
May the energy of the Buddha embrace me.
May the Pure Land manifest.
Please bring the torch of understanding
and shine it upon my mind.
Please carry me on your boat of long lifespan
so that I can live with peace and joy,
and my ideal can be fulfilled.
May the Buddha always protect me,
so that my mind is not heedless.
May I put an end to wrong views
and leave behind the afflictions.
In the present moment
the Buddha is in my life.
In every step
I can enter the Pure Land, solid and free.
When I live the present moment mindfully,
the Pure Land is already a reality,
and when I manifest in different forms,
there will also be peace and joy.
[BELL]

Recollecting Amitabha Buddha
with an undispersed mind,
the nine grades of lotus appear.
Without distinguishing self and other,
we receive the fruit of the practice.
We know in advance the time of our death.
Our mind does not flinch,
our body is not in pain,
and there is no thought of hesitation.
Amitabha with his holy sangha,
holding the golden lotus,
is present without delay,
and together we continue on the path in freedom.
The lotus opens and we see the Buddha.
The Pure Land is our true home.

We bow our heads and ask the Buddha
to witness our diligent practice.
[BELL, BELL]

CHANT OF PRAISE AND ASPIRATION

The udumbara flower is still present.
Its five petals emit a wonderfully subtle fragrance.
The Dharma treasure transmitted from India
continued in the Mind-Seal school in China and further east.
May you our ancestral teachers of all generations,
residing in the nirvana of the wonderful mind,
be seated high on the precious Dharma throne,
and with the awakened understanding
which transcends the suffering of the world,
look down on your descendants.
Please be compassionate witnesses to our aspiration:
You our ancestral teachers have opened up
the path of stability and freedom.
You are the example and source of inspiration for all future generations.

We, your descendants in (*insert the name of your practice center and the
country: e.g. Plum Village, south-western France*)
have gathered as a Fourfold Sangha.
We have come into the meditation hall before the altar,
to practice meditation and reciting the sutras,
to praise the actions and virtues of our respected ancestral teachers.
With whole-hearted respect and sincerity
we want to express our deep gratitude.

We touch the earth before you the bodhisattvas,
our ancestral teachers from India and the Far East,
the teachers who founded our root temple,
and all the generations of teachers who preceded them
and have opened up the way of practice for us, your descendants.
We are determined to practice steadfastly
to transform the afflictions,
to nourish our bodhicitta,
so that the lineage school may remain strong and alive,

and the seal of our ancestral teachers grow clearer and brighter,
so that the flowers of awakening bloom everywhere
in the forest of meditation,
and the rain of the wonderful teachings penetrates our place of practice.
We, your disciples, grateful for the teachings of our ancestral teachers,
vow to accept each other, forgive each other,
and love each other as children of the same family,
in order to strengthen the sangha body,
so that happiness can be assured
and we can be a place of refuge for countless beings in the ten directions.
May we follow in the footsteps of Mahakashyapa, Ananda, Nagarjuna,
Aryadeva, Asanga and Vasubandhu, Master Linji and Master Liễu Quán,
as well as all other dragons and elephants of the meditation school,
and all those who have aspired to great action,
all the bodhisattva mahasattvas
and the insight that brings us to the other shore.
[BELL, BELL]

Monastics and visitors practice the art of mindful living in the tradition of Thich Nhat Hanh at our mindfulness practice centers around the world. To reach any of these communities, or for information about how individuals, couples, and families can join in a retreat, please contact:

Plum Village
33580 Dieulivol, France
plumvillage.org

Magnolia Grove Monastery
Batesville, MS 38606, USA
magnoliagrovemonastery.org

Blue Cliff Monastery
Pine Bush, NY 12566, USA
bluecliffmonastery.org

Deer Park Monastery
Escondido, CA 92026, USA
deerparkmonastery.org

European Institute of Applied Buddhism
D-51545 Waldbröl, Germany
eiab.eu

Thailand Plum Village
Nakhon Ratchasima
30130 Thailand
thaiplumvillage.org

Asian Institute of Applied Buddhism
Ngong Ping
Lantau Island, Hong Kong
pvfhk.org

Maison de l'Inspir
77510 Villeneuve-sur-Bellot
France
maisondelinspir.org

Healing Spring Monastery
77510 Verdelot, France
healingspringmonastery.org

Nhap Luu–Stream Entering Monastery
Porcupine Ridge
Victoria 3461, Australia.
nhapluu.org

Mountain Spring Monastery
Bilpin, NSW 2758, Australia
mountainspringmonastery.org

THICH NHAT HANH FOUNDATION

planting seeds of Compassion

The Thich Nhat Hanh Foundation works to continue the mindful teachings and practice of Zen Master Thich Nhat Hanh, in order to foster peace and transform suffering in all people, animals, plants, and our planet. Through donations to the Foundation, thousands of generous supporters ensure the continuation of Plum Village practice centers and monastics around the world, bring transformative practices to those who otherwise would not be able to access them, support local mindfulness initiatives, and bring humanitarian relief to communities in crisis in Vietnam.

By becoming a supporter, you join many others who want to learn and share these life-changing practices of mindfulness, loving speech, deep listening, and compassion for oneself, each other, and the planet.

For more information on how you can help support mindfulness around the world, or to subscribe to the Foundation's monthly newsletter with teachings, news, and global retreats, **visit tnhf.org.**

**PARALLAX
PRESS**

Parallax Press, a nonprofit publisher founded by
Zen Master Thich Nhat Hanh, publishes books and media
on the art of mindful living and Engaged Buddhism.
We are committed to offering teachings that help transform
suffering and injustice. Our aspiration is to contribute
to collective insight and awakening, bringing about a
more joyful, healthy, and compassionate society.

Parallax Press
P.O. Box 7355
Berkeley, CA 94707
parallax.org

The Mindfulness Bell, a journal of the art of mindful living in the tradition
of Thich Nhat Hanh, is published two times a year by our community.
To subscribe or to see the worldwide directory of Sanghas
(local mindfulness groups), visit **mindfulnessbell.org**.